verse mapping

— BIBLE STUDY —

Acts

FEASTING ON THE ABUNDANCE OF GOD'S WORD

STUDY GUIDE | SIX SESSIONS

KRISTY CAMBRON

THOMAS NELSON

Since 1798

Verse Mapping Bible Study
Acts: Feasting on the Abundance of God's Word

© 2018 by Kristy Cambron

Published in Nashville, Tennessee, by Thomas Nelson. Thomas Nelson is a registered trademark of HarperCollins Christian Publishing, Inc.

Published in association with Books & Such Literary Management, 52 Mission Circle, Suite 122, PMB 170, Santa Rosa, California 95409-5370, www.booksandsuch.com.

Thomas Nelson titles may be purchased in bulk for educational, business, fundraising, or sales promotional use. For information, please e-mail SpecialMarkets@ThomasNelson.com.

ISBN 978-0-310-09001-4

First Printing March 2018 / Printed in the United States of America

Contents

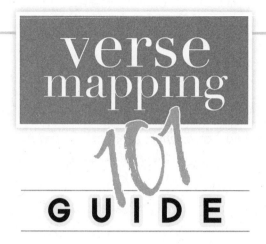

verse mapping 101

G U I D E

Steps to Study the Bible
Like Never Before

WHY VERSE MAPPING?

Let's be honest—does anyone else have difficulty understanding Scripture? *(Waving hand over here . . .)*

Do you want to do more than just read—you actually want to research and apply what's in the Bible to your life today? *(Me too! Waving again.)*

Are you looking for a fellowship community where you can read, learn, explore, and map the Word of God together? *(Still here!)*

If this is you too, and you love unpacking the context of the Scriptures you're reading, but you want to do it in a super-simple way—looking at the Hebrew/Greek translations, finding connections in the Word, and learning as much as you can from your time with the Holy Spirit—then get ready. . . . You've just joined the community study that will inspire, encourage, and unlock your understanding of the Word of God!

WHAT IS VERSE MAPPING?

Verse mapping isn't new. It's been a topic of conversation for years. You'll find endless examples with a simple online search. And you guessed it—Bible journaling images and methods are popping up all over social media. But what is verse mapping? Who's doing it? And can it really help you understand the Word more clearly?

First things first . . .

definition: *Verse mapping is a method of studying the historical context, transliteration, translation, connotation, and theological framework of a verse (or section of verses) in the Bible.*

Plain and simple? Verse mapping is getting real about studying the Bible. All of it. It's not just reading. It's researching everything you can in a verse to learn more about who God is and how He wants to speak to you through His Word. In short? It's serious study.

④ *actions* What actions develop the story in this verse? What is happening in this verse? To whom?

① *verse* What verse am I mapping? What key themes or specific words are speaking to me today?

② *design* What different translations make up the design for this verse? Underline key phrases or words repeated.

develop ③ What is the Hebrew or Greek meaning for the underlined phrases or words?

⑤ *outcome* What is God saying to me today? How do I apply this to my life?

HOW-TO FOR BEGINNERS

What qualifies me to do this kind of study?

If you're not a seminary-trained theologian by education, don't worry—verse mapping is for anyone with a heart to know the Word of God more.

What matters is not how much knowledge you have before you begin, but where the experience takes you. Verse mapping will inspire you to dig into the Word of God in individual study and in a group setting like never before. The Holy Spirit is your teacher and companion in this study; it's not the *what* you bring to the table that qualifies you—it's *Who*. And He's going to make sure you learn no matter where you begin.

What are the rules?

- **Rule #1:** If you can't back up your conclusions or thoughts with Scripture, then you can't write it down. Everything is fair game in studying *as long as God said it first.* (In other words, don't make anything up and don't assume you know what something means— back it up with Scripture or go back and find the *real* answer.)

- **Rule #2:** Make it personal. This is your journal and your study time with God. More than anything, let God meet you in this unique and intimate space and speak to you.

- **Rule #3:** Keep to your preferences for verse mapping—if you like to highlight . . . if you like to use a specific marker/pen color . . . or if you like to circle or underline key words and phrases. Do what feels intuitive for you.

There's no structurally right or wrong way to verse map. This particular study is structured working from right to left (a documentation page on the right, notes page on the left), and top to bottom. Once you've gathered the tools and mastered the confidence to apply what you've learned, it's up to you how your journal will look. Focus on the process and the way of this study method. Learn how to read and ask at the same time, and then go find the answers.

GATHERING AND GETTING STARTED

This section is quick. It's all about gathering a handful of tools and readying your heart for Him.

What you will need

Whether you're at a desk in your home office, at the local coffee shop, or on the go, verse mapping is a study method that will move with you. In fact, you probably already carry everything you need just about anywhere you go:

- **Journal:** Verse Mapping study guide with blank maps, or a notebook with blank pages.

- **Markers/pens:** Specific colors of markers or pens aren't required. This is personal.

- **Bible:** Or a Bible app on a smart device (to look up various translations).

- **Concordance:** Select a concordance with Hebrew/Greek dictionaries. I recommend *The NIV Exhaustive Bible Concordance, Third Edition* from Zondervan, but you can also find the information online. If you don't have one—or if you're not able to carry one with you—you can also find this information on your smart device.

- **Time (varies):** While it's a requirement, the time you block on your calendar is *up to you.* Study time is on the honor system between you and God. If you have five minutes today and an hour tomorrow, dedicate what time you can, when you can. It's all about communion with Him.

Study Prompt:

Time is a big factor. You may have others who depend on you either inside your home, outside it, or both—and that can cut into the time you're able to study. If finding study *time* is a struggle that becomes a burden, then add that into the next step and pray about it. Eventually, you won't have to carve out time in the Word; it will be what your heart craves first, and most. The time to study will follow the passion to learn.

Prayer

This is a Holy Spirit-led study. So pray. Talk to Him. Ask Him to reveal more of who He is through your verse mapping journey.

The Holy Spirit must be the active guide in any time of study. Do whatever works to invite Him into your study space (listen to worship music, close the door, turn off all sound). Pray before every single time you open your Bible and intentionally seek deeper and clearer understanding of what you will read.

MAPPING 101

A comprehensive guide to change-your-life study time with God.

The process is simple. Each of the following words corresponds to a section on your verse map. Here's what you do (after you pray!):

- **Verse:** Select and write your verse(s) to map. Include the translation.

- **Design:** Write your verse(s) in two to four different translations. Identify key words or phrases that stand out among the varying translations.

- **Develop:** Look up key words or phrases in Hebrew/Greek. Write down definitions, synonyms, and root words. Discover any underlying meaning(s) in verse(s) and note it. (See the Reference and Resource Guide at the back of this study guide if you need help with where to look words up.)

- **Actions:** Research and document the people, places, and the context referenced. Ask: Who? What? Where? When? Why? How? Note connections to other concepts in Scripture you are familiar with and/or find in your research.

- **Outcome:** Write a one- to two-sentence summary of what you've learned. Anchor the verse you mapped to your life. This is the treasured truth the map brought you to.

That's it—five simple steps to change-your-life study time with God! All set? Let's map.

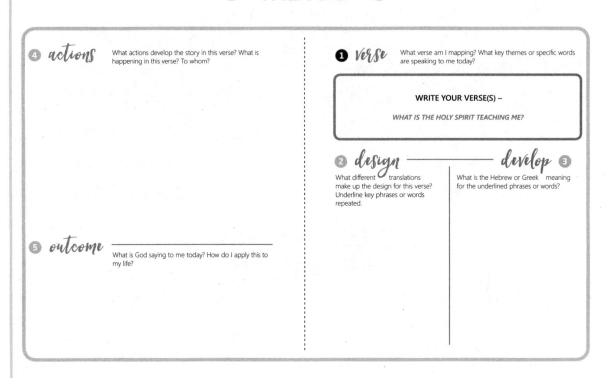

⟩ THE MAP ⟨

4 actions
What actions develop the story in this verse? What is happening in this verse? To whom?

1 verse
What verse am I mapping? What key themes or specific words are speaking to me today?

WRITE YOUR VERSE(S) –

WHAT IS THE HOLY SPIRIT TEACHING ME?

2 design ———— **develop 3**

What different translations make up the design for this verse? Underline key phrases or words repeated.

What is the Hebrew or Greek meaning for the underlined phrases or words?

5 outcome _____
What is God saying to me today? How do I apply this to my life?

1 verse

Select your verse(s)

Everything in your map will hinge on what verse(s) you select. Whether you're reading through an entire book of the Bible or moving around through a verse(s) of a specific theme, this is where you choose what your path will be for your study time. A few questions to ask yourself as you read:

- *What grabs me when I read it?*

- *What themes do I see?*

- *What question(s) do I have about what I just read?*

Write your verse(s)

If something stands out, then you can be sure that's your verse(s) for the day. Select it and write it down.

This study is formatted for use with the New International Version of the Bible. However, you can choose which translation(s) you prefer most. Once you've selected the verse(s) you'll map, write it in your preferred translation. (Remember, you'll document it in at least two to four other translations next.)

Study Prompt:

What verse are you mapping? What key themes or specific words are speaking to you today?

- *What's on your heart today?* If you're facing a difficult circumstance, or find yourself in an unexpected path in your own story with God, select a verse(s) that speaks to the theme of your heart for today.

- *What's that word?* If you're reading Scripture and something jumps off the page—a word you don't recognize, a city you've never heard of, or a phrase you don't quite understand—this is a good indication it might be your verse(s) to map for the day.

Everything in your map will hinge on what verse(s) you select.

Study Prompt:

What gets lost in translation? How do the different translations present the same ideas or biblical principles?

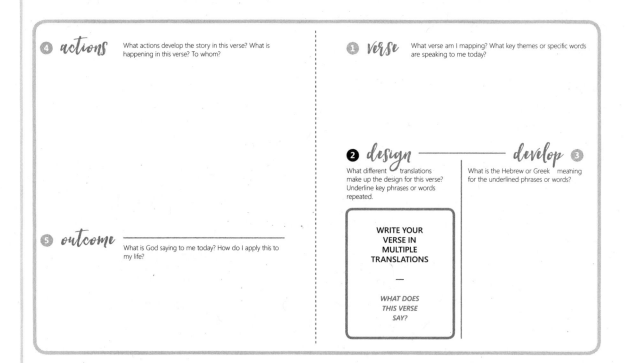

4 actions What actions develop the story in this verse? What is happening in this verse? To whom?

1 verse What verse am I mapping? What key themes or specific words are speaking to me today?

2 design ———————— **develop 3**

What different translations make up the design for this verse? Underline key phrases or words repeated.

What is the Hebrew or Greek meaning for the underlined phrases or words?

WRITE YOUR VERSE IN MULTIPLE TRANSLATIONS

—

WHAT DOES THIS VERSE SAY?

5 outcome _____
What is God saying to me today? How do I apply this to my life?

2 design

The *design* identifies what the verse is calling attention to by comparing translations. The *design* calls out similar word choice, repetition of words, phrases, and/or aspects of grammar common across multiple translations. It brings to light what the verse is saying that cannot be lost to translation, and what may stand out as translation specific. Anything here could trigger a question or path for further investigation.

Write your verse(s)—or selected phrase(s)—in two to four additional translations. Underline, circle, or highlight key phrases or words that may be repeated across multiple translations.

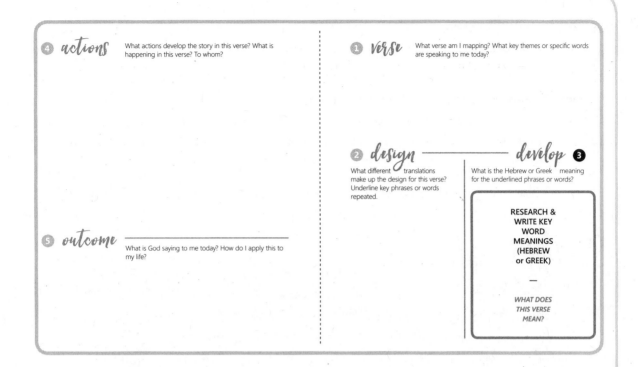

❹ *actions* What actions develop the story in this verse? What is happening in this verse? To whom?

❶ *verse* What verse am I mapping? What key themes or specific words are speaking to me today?

❷ *design* —————— *develop* ❸

What different translations make up the design for this verse? Underline key phrases or words repeated.

What is the Hebrew or Greek meaning for the underlined phrases or words?

> RESEARCH & WRITE KEY WORD MEANINGS (HEBREW or GREEK)
>
> —
>
> *WHAT DOES THIS VERSE MEAN?*

❺ *outcome* What is God saying to me today? How do I apply this to my life?

❸ *develop*

Develop why and how the verse, key word(s), or idea is important through Hebrew (Old Testament) or Greek (New Testament) word research, definitions, and comparisons. Dig deeper. Use a concordance and online word search databases. Look up the meanings of your key words or phrases and write them down.

Note word choice, part(s) of speech, and find some seriously cool context around your verse.

If a word is used across all translations, find out why. If the verse moves from past tense (something that's already happened) to present tense (something that's ongoing), find out why. If a Greek word was used in one translation and not another . . . find out why.

- **Old Testament verses**—research the Hebrew.

  Example: S. 6213. *asah* (aw-saw) a primitive root; to do or make, in the broadest sense and widest application (as follows):—accomplish, advance, appoint

- **New Testament verses**—research the Greek.

  Example: S. 4100. *pisteuó* (pist-yoo′-o) from 4102; to have faith (in, upon, or with respect to, a person or thing), i.e. credit; by implication, to entrust (especially one's spiritual well-being to Christ):—believe(-r), commit (to trust), put in trust with

  Note: S. is an abbreviation for *The NIV Exhaustive Concordance.*

Study Prompt:

Look at the verse in context. Think like a storyteller—how would you explain what's happening in your verse? Find the five senses in the story—sight, smell, sound, taste, and touch—as if you stepped into the characters' shoes. Look at what occurred before and after your verse. What's happening that caused the action in your verse?

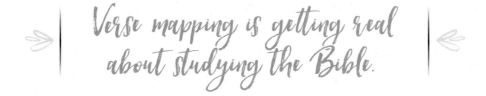

Verse mapping is getting real about studying the Bible.

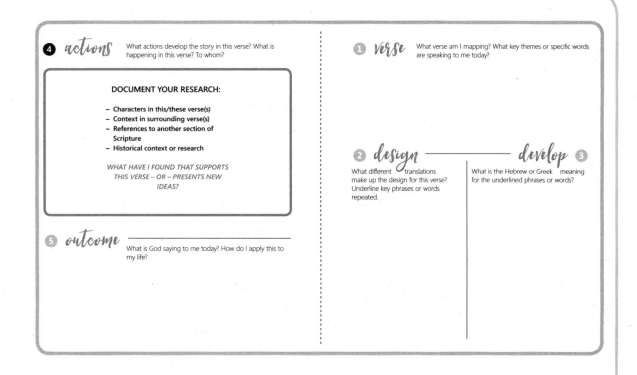

4 actions

Actions record:

- What's happening in the verse

- Who the characters are in what you're reading

- How their story relates to other stories/verses/persons in other areas of Scripture

- What are the topics, themes, dates of significant events, and/or theological elements of the verse(s) you're researching

Anything is fair game here, as long as you can back it up with Scripture. Look back a few chapters or verses and read what precedes your verse(s). Identify who, what, where, when. Research the context and customs of what life would have been like for the characters in your verse(s). Look up maps. Open history books. Read about what happened, why it happened, and how it is relevant to your life today.

This is where you'll find how the story connects to *your* story with God. Research it and write it down.

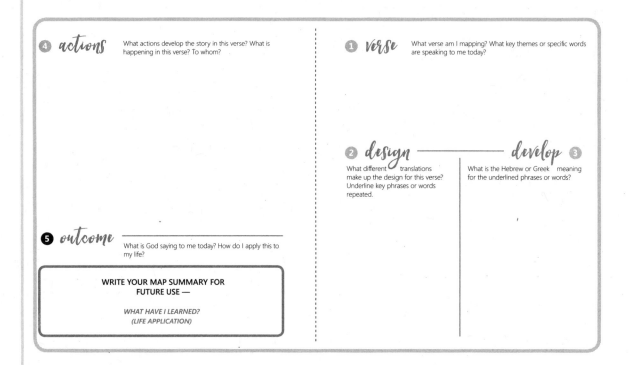

⑤ outcome

The *outcome* is a quick-hit summary of what you've learned. One or two sentences should do it. Summarize, jot it down, and come back later to find where the Holy Spirit has confirmed His promises to you. This is your claim on this verse, at this time of your life. The *outcome* should reflect whatever truth has been revealed in your map.

Study Prompt:

As you continue verse mapping, you'll find this is the section that you refer back to most often. Summarize what you've learned—how would you take this truth and apply it in your home, office, school, church, or community? Make it short and powerful.

SPECIAL NOTE

Don't be afraid to start small.

If your first maps are one or two pages with lots of white space, that's okay. Other maps (depending on what you need to hear from God that day) could turn into four pages of study that digs deep into your heart.

Look up a word here. Choose a verse there. Just do it honestly, and the Holy Spirit will grow your passion around His Word. You don't have to have it all figured out with the first or even the twentieth map. You just have to come hungry to the table every day. God will handle the preparation for the feast ahead of time.

So, now it's your turn! Want to give it a try? Join the *community* of other Jesus-chasing mappers out there. Be sure to use the hashtag #VerseMapClub to connect and share your verse-map experience on social media. I'll be adding more posts soon, and you can bet I'll want to see how it's going for you. Connect with me on social media—I'm heart-happy to take this journey with you!

Acts

The Fellowship

When the day of Pentecost came, they were all together
in one place. Suddenly a sound like the blowing of a violent wind
came from heaven and filled the whole house where they were sitting.
They saw what seemed to be tongues of fire that separated and came
to rest on each of them. All of them were filled with the Holy Spirit
and began to speak in other tongues as the Spirit enabled them.

ACTS 2:1–4

OPENING REFLECTION

The book of Acts is a portrait of COMMUNITY + UNITY. The fellowship of the early church—
and the believers who gathered—show us we were never meant to walk our faith journey
alone. And because of the actions of the Holy Spirit in an upper room, believers gathered
around a feast table were forever changed.

What if we could learn God's promises, understand, and apply the Word in our community, believing the feast makes us stronger? Verse mapping is just that; it's thriving in community, pulling out a chair at the table made ready for every heart to unlock the feast of God's
Word.

What if we were never meant to walk our faith journey alone?

FEASTING AND GETTING STARTED

Welcome to the first session of *Acts: Feasting on the Abundance of God's Word.*

Whether you've gathered in a favorite coffee shop corner, a church fellowship hall, in your home, or even on your neighbor's porch, this is meant to be a *feasting study.* The book of Acts is perfect for a verse mapping journey like this, because at its core, it's all about two things:

- *The thriving COMMUNITY of the newly formed church—its beginnings and the gospel's spread from Jerusalem to Rome,*

- *And still a part of that word COMMUNITY—the believer's UNITY with the Holy Spirit.*

This is our invitation to the table—to talk faith, life, and story roads—to pull out a chair at the place set for us and invite the Holy Spirit into our every day.

If this is the first time you've gathered together, take a few moments to get to know your group. Introduce yourself with something as simple as your name and why you've come to study God's Word. And if you want to jump in to get things started, discuss the following questions:

- *What do you know about verse mapping? What do you hope to learn on this verse mapping journey?*

- *What's your biggest barrier to overcome in studying God's Word? Is it a lack of time? Knowledge? Or something else?*

FEASTING: VIDEO STORY

Play the video segment for session one. As you watch the first video, follow the verse mapping guide points starting on the next page and refer to the completed map on pages 24–25. Take brief notes or record questions that might lead you to further research in your independent study time this week.

Notes

1 *verse*

What makes the book of Acts (Acts of the Apostles) unique:

Out of twenty-seven books in the New Testament—the Gospels (Matthew to John), the Acts of the Apostles, Paul's letters (Romans to Philemon), the remaining general letters (Hebrews to Jude), and a book of prophecy known as Revelation—Acts is the outlier as we place categories to the books

Acts is the only sequel written by a Gospel author (Luke 1:3; Acts 1:1) and the only book (with the Gospel of Luke) to offer a detailed account of Jesus' ascension

In the book of Acts, Luke builds a foundation of faith for the early church—based on accounts of Jesus' majesty and authority, His atoning death and resurrection, and the arrival and empowering work of the Holy Spirit in the lives of believers (Acts 2:1–4)

2 *design*

There are two defined acts of the Holy Spirit in this passage: "the blowing of a violent wind," and the "tongues of fire that separated and came to rest" on all those in the room

The New King James Version describes "a rushing of mighty wind" and "divided tongues, as of fire"

Other translations: "a sound like a strong wind, gale force" (MSG) and "a violent, rushing wind" (NASB). And of the fire, these translations describe it as "what seemed to be tongues of fire" (MSG) and "tongues of fire, distributing themselves" (NASB).

Violent wind FILLED the room and then the disciples were FILLED with the Holy Spirit. The Holy Spirit FILLED the COMMUNITY—and each believer—to individual completion.

❸ *develop*

In the Greek, *pléroó* (S. 4137) [S. is an abbreviation for *The NIV Exhaustive Concordance*] is used to describe the violent rush of breath in the room, meaning "to fill or amply supply; to complete, or fill to individual capacity"

In the Greek, the word used for "fire" is *pýr* (S. 4442), meaning "fire, a spark or flame." It's used figuratively here, describing God's Spirit as a holy fire, light or lightning, or an eternal flame.

In the Greek, *glóssa* (S. 1100) means "speech or language." The believers in the upper room were each made individually complete . . . by the BREATH of GOD filling their lungs . . . to thereafter speak the LANGUAGE of LIGHT.

❹ *actions*

Holy Spirit's ACTIONS to establish the church:

Violent wind FILLED the upper room (Acts 2:2)

Disciples were FILLED with the Holy Spirit (Acts 2:3–4)

Holy Spirit FILLED the COMMUNITY—and each believer—to individual completion (Acts 2:4)

Resulting actions:

"Every nation" of those gathered hear the rush of WIND (Acts 2:5)

Crowds are "utterly amazed" to hear disciples speaking foreign TONGUES (Acts 2:7)

Peter stands up to explain what is happening—some three thousand people come to believe in Christ that day (Acts 2:40–41)

5 *outcome*

Acts is a portrait of COMMUNITY among believers + UNITY with the Holy Spirit. We have the same access to the Holy Spirit that the disciples did, and the same empowering actions for the church to grow.

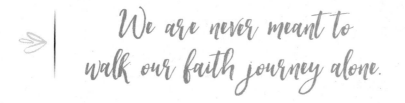

We are never meant to walk our faith journey alone.

 **4** *actions*

What if we were never meant to walk our faith journey alone?

Holy Spirit's ACTIONS to establish the church—

- *Violent wind FILLED the upper room* (Acts 2:2)

- *Disciples were FILLED with the Holy Spirit* (Acts 2:3–4)

- *Holy Spirit FILLED the COMMUNITY—and each believer—to individual completion* (Acts 2:4)

Resulting actions—

- *"every nation" of those gathered hear the rush of WIND* (Acts 2:5)

- *Crowds are "utterly amazed" to hear disciples speaking foreign TONGUES* (Acts 2:7)

- *Peter stands up to explain what is happening—some 3,000 people come to believe in Christ that day* (Acts 2:40–41)

5 *outcome*

Acts is a portrait of COMMUNITY among believers + UNITY with the Holy Spirit. We have the same access to the Holy Spirit that the disciples did; and the same empowering actions for the church to grow.

① *verse*   ACTS 2:1–4 (NIV)

When the day of Pentecost came, they were all together in one place. Suddenly a sound like the <u>blowing of a violent wind</u> came from heaven and filled the whole house where they were sitting. They saw what seemed to be <u>tongues of fire</u> that separated and came to rest on each of them. All of them were filled with the Holy Spirit and began to speak in other tongues as the Spirit enabled them.

② *design* ———————— *develop* ③

NKJV: *"And suddenly there came a sound from heaven, as of a <u>rushing mighty wind</u> . . . Then there appeared to them <u>divided tongues, as of fire</u> . . ."*

- **WIND**—*pnoé* (S. 4157):

  "wind"—but wind that comes as a BREATH; a respiration breeze, with gale-force strength

- **FILLED**—*pléroó* (S. 4137):

  "to fill or amply supply; to complete, or fill to individual capacity"

- **FIRE**—*pýr (S. 4442):*

  "fire; a spark or flame." Used figuratively: "God's Spirit—a holy fire, light or lightning, or an eternal flame"

- **TONGUES**—*glóssa (S. 1100):*

  "speech or language"

From the Video

I took a deep breath and walked into the women's Bible study. The fellowship hall was packed with more than a hundred women. Smiling faces were everywhere, and cheery voices created a hum in the air. The women carried Bibles and notebooks. I watched as they hugged at the donut table and caught up over cups of coffee I could smell lingering in the air. Everyone seemed energized about this fellowship thing called "Bible Study."

I stopped and stood in the back of the room, feeling a little intimidated because I didn't know anyone. A crippling thought kept running through my mind: How was I going to hide the fact that I didn't always understand the Bible? Instead of being excited, I wanted to turn around and run out of that room. (But I didn't. I stayed.)

 Jesus appeared to disciples after His crucifixion and opened the Scriptures to them. "He said to them, 'How foolish you are, and how slow to believe all that the prophets have spoken! Did not the Messiah have to suffer these things and then enter his glory?' And beginning with Moses and all the Prophets, he explained to them what was said in all the Scriptures concerning himself" (Luke 24:25–27).

FEAST TABLE: DISCUSSION

Take a few moments with your group to discuss the video you just watched and explore these concepts in Scripture.

1. Think about Luke's documentation of events that led to the birth of the church in Jerusalem, around AD 30–35. How does he use these accounts to paint a detailed portrait of our heritage as believers? Starting out on this faith journey, do you think the members of

the early church could have envisioned the message of the gospel traveling from Jerusalem, to Judea and Samaria, and eventually all the way to Rome?

2. Select a volunteer (or more than one) to read Luke 3:16, John 4:1–2, and Acts 1:7–8 aloud to the group. How do these verses foretell the arrival and actions of the Holy Spirit seen in Acts 2:1–4? What kind of authority does the Holy Spirit bring to believers?

3. Select a diferent volunteer to read Acts 2:14–38 aloud to the group. How long did the Holy Spirit wait before enabling Peter to speak out—in this, his first public sermon? Are we empowered by the Holy Spirit to speak out and share the gospel in the same way?

4. When we put our faith in Jesus, His Holy Spirit breathes life into our lungs and baptizes our tongues. How does the Holy Spirit bring individual UNITY to each of us, and cultivate a COMMUNITY of believers?

Define "fellowship." How is fellowship different from community? What do these mean to you?

_____

_____

_____

_____

How important is community in the life of a believer?

_____

_____

_____

FEAST TABLE: GROUP ACTIVITY

For this activity, each participant will need a Bible, pens/markers, and a smart device (such as a phone or tablet).

- Using a Bible or Bible app on a smart device, look up two additional translations of Acts 2:1–4, and then record them on the completed map on pages 24–25.

- To start your verse mapping journey, pray as a group and select one verse you'll map from Acts 1–2 in individual study time this week. Gather in Week 2 and discuss how your map is the same or differed from others' maps.

FEAST TABLE: CLOSING PRAYER

If you've gathered for a verse mapping study before, you know the experience begins and ends with prayer.

Today we gather around the table with open hearts, expecting the Holy Spirit to breathe life into this space, and as we pray, to open the Word of God in us like never before.

SESSION

INDIVIDUAL STUDY

The Fellowship

When the day of Pentecost came, they were all together in one place. Suddenly a sound like the blowing of a violent wind came from heaven and filled the whole house where they were sitting. They saw what seemed to be tongues of fire that separated and came to rest on each of them. All of them were filled with the Holy Spirit and began to speak in other tongues as the Spirit enabled them.

ACTS 2:1–4

We're in the same COMMUNITY today as those in the upper room. We have the same Holy Spirit and the same opportunity to cultivate His church. We've also pulled our chair up to the FEAST table, "hands out," carrying all our FEARS and FAILURES, with intimidated FAITH and cracks in the FOUNDATION of our beliefs. And we're PRAYING to know what to do, just like those early believers.

FEAST: INDIVIDUAL STUDY INVITATION

Fellowship. Followers. New believers and spiritual family . . .

The book is called the Acts of the Apostles—but by now, you're learning the acts outlined in its pages shine a spotlight not just on the early believers but more so on the miraculous outworking of the Holy Spirit. That's the invitation you'll find in Acts 1–2: to step into an upper room with Him (1:12–14); to engage in the promise that He'll meet you there (1:7–8) and immediately qualify you with authority for far greater things than you could have ever imagined (2:14).

Breathe in—that's His respiration breath enveloping you as you explore (2:1–2).

Dwell in—that's His presence completing you as you study (2:3–4).

Remove the words "I can't" from your vocabulary. Because with the Holy Spirit—in constant, power-laden, authentic fellowship—you find the shift you've been waiting for in your own story. And like Peter who immediately steps out of the upper room to find any former shred of meekness has been replaced with boldness, you'll find you're qualified by and in Him alone (2:14).

When the day of Pentecost came, they were all together in one place. Suddenly a sound like the blowing of a violent wind came from heaven and filled the whole house where they were sitting. They saw what seemed to be tongues of fire that separated and came to rest on each of them. All of them were filled with the Holy Spirit and began to speak in other tongues as the Spirit enabled them.
(ACTS 2:1–4)

Gather

INDIVIDUAL STUDY SUPPORT

If this is your first time verse mapping, you may need a couple of prompts to get started. Or refer back to the Verse Mapping 101 Guide at the beginning of your study guide.

1 *verse*   What verse am I mapping? What key themes or specific words are speaking to me today?

2 *design*   What different translations make up the design for this verse? Underline key phrases or words that are repeated across different translations.

3 *develop*   What is the Hebrew or Greek meaning for the underlined phrases or words?

4 *actions*   What actions develop the story in this verse? What is happening in this verse? To whom?

5 *outcome*   Review your map from beginning to end. Notice what God is saying to you through the verse map. How does your life apply to your life?

Read
⇒ ACTS 1 — 2 ⇐

Take time this week, whether five minutes today or an hour tomorrow, to live out that prayer. And see what happens next. See how the BREATH of WIND and the TONGUES of FIRE empower you to dive into God's Word.

Pray and invite the Holy Spirit into your time in the Word. When you are ready, turn to one of the blank verse maps in this section.

Read Acts 1–2. Select and map a verse that speaks to your heart. If your group selected a verse to map and discuss together, map that verse this week as well. Prepare to discuss what you've learned when your group gathers again.

He's called you to discipleship . . . time to descend the stairs.

Study Prompt

Look at the verse in context. Think like a storyteller—how would you explain what's happening in your verse? Find the five senses in the story—sight, smell, sound, taste, and touch—as if you stepped into the characters' shoes. Look at what occurred before and after your verse. What's happening that caused the action in your verse?

Study Support Examples

Information you might find in your research . . .

Themes and Theology: 1. *The mission and the messengers.* If the Gospel of Luke is about "all that Jesus began to do and to teach" (Acts 1:1), Acts is about what Jesus continues to do through his disciples in the power of the Spirit. The role of the disciples is to be Jesus' "witnesses" (1:8), his representatives. Acts 1:8 represents both the central theme of the book (the unstoppable progress of the gospel) and its general outline: beginning in Jerusalem and moving outward in concentric circles through Judea, Samaria, and to the ends of the earth. The traditional title of the book, "the Acts of the Apostles," fails to reflect accurately the book's contents, since the 12 apostles play a relatively minor role. The main human characters, like Peter, Barnabas, Stephen, Philip, and Paul, play a central role not because of their *status* as apostles but because of their *function* in breaking down barriers to the advance of the gospel. Acts is fundamentally about the mission of the church and the progress of salvation from its Jewish roots to the Gentile world.

The Spirit Empowers the Church for Witness (1:1–2:47)

A. Jesus Taken Up Into Heaven (1:1–11)

B. Matthias Chosen to Replace Judas (1:12-26)

C. The Events on the Day of Pentecost (2:1–47)

   1. The Holy Spirit Comes at Pentecost (2:1–13)

   2. Peter Addresses the Crowd (2:14–41)

   3. The Fellowship of the Believers (2:42–47)

Excerpted from *NIV Biblical Theology Study Bible*. Copyright © 2015, 2018, Zondervan.

4 *actions*

What actions develop the story in this verse? What is happening in this verse? To whom?

5 *outcome*

What is God saying to me today? How do I apply this to my life?

1 *verse*

What verse am I mapping? What key themes or specific words are speaking to me today?

2 *design* ——————————— *develop* **3**

What different translations make up the design for this verse? Underline key phrases or words repeated.

What is the Hebrew or Greek meaning for the underlined phrases or words?

4 *actions*

What actions develop the story in this verse? What is happening in this verse? To whom?

5 *outcome*

What is God saying to me today? How do I apply this to my life?

1 *verse* — What verse am I mapping? What key themes or specific words are speaking to me today?

2 *design* —————————————— *develop* **3**

What different translations make up the design for this verse? Underline key phrases or words repeated.

What is the Hebrew or Greek meaning for the underlined phrases or words?

The Unseen

Now a man who was lame from birth was being carried to the temple gate called Beautiful. . . . Peter looked straight at him, as did John. Then Peter said, "Look at us!" So the man gave them his attention, expecting to get something from them. Then Peter said, "Silver or gold I do not have, but what I do have I give to you. In the name of Jesus Christ of Nazareth, walk."

ACTS 3:2, 4–6

OPENING REFLECTION

The idea of being KNOWN is a key theme in this week's study of Acts. In a story of the unseen, unknown, and passed by, Peter and John change everything for this man. For the man, this one interaction builds a foundation of faith within him and confirms the promise that he is KNOWN by God. As we continue our story, it's the broken and forgotten who encounter a Savior. The unknown find a home. The unnamed are finally given one. And those who thought they were unseemly and unattractive are at once called "Beautiful."

What if, despite the demands of my schedule, time, responsibilities, needs, desires, and dreams, I am still known by God? Am I seen even when I don't see Him? This week becomes that story, of the unseen being seen by God Himself.

What if the God we didn't know, already knows us?

FEASTING AND GETTING STARTED

Welcome back to session two of *Acts: Feasting on the Abundance of God's Word*.

We've gathered for a second time—realizing that the Holy Spirit who enabled the disciples in the upper room is the same who will enable us to study in a new, in-depth, and possibly more vulnerable way.

To start, let's talk heart. After your first week in verse mapping, discuss the following in group share:

● *What verse(s) did you select to map, and why? How did it go?*

   or

● *What moments of faith-stretching did you experience in self-study time this week—did it take a step of faith to embrace a new approach to studying the Word? Where did your exploration take you?*

FEASTING: VIDEO STORY

Play the video segment for session two. As you watch the next installment of our book of Acts story, follow the verse mapping guide points starting on the next page and refer to the completed map on pages 44–45. Take brief notes or record questions that might lead you to further research in your independent study time this week.

Do you consider yourself seen?

Notes

1 *verse*

What stands out in these verses:

> The lame man asks for alms without even looking at a proposed benefactor. Peter has to tell him to look up—the man does, but is still reluctant.

> Peter and John—and, by extension, the Holy Spirit—stop to make this man KNOWN. They're healing the sick and wounded places of his heart—building the foundation of his faith first.

> Healing the man goes from healed faith—with the Holy Spirit leading the charge—to the healing of his broken body too

2 *design*

> New King James Version states "and [Peter] fixing his eyes on him, with John" ... and of the beggar it says, "So he gave them his attention."

> Other translations: The beggar "asked for a handout," and "Peter, with John at his side, looked him straight in the eye and said, 'Look here'" (MSG). The beggar "began to give them his attention, expecting to receive something from them" (NASB).

③ develop

In the Greek, *blepó* (S. 991) means "to look, see, or discern." The word choice suggests to see something physical with the eyes, and find spiritual results from it.

In the Greek, *hóraios* (S. 5611) means "fair or beautiful," and "blooming." Figuratively, it means something has developed and become beautiful in an appointed "season" of time, or something is fruitful because it's fully developed.

The lame man laying outside the temple doorway—his body never fully developed from his mother's womb—is in stark contrast to this truly picturesque gate. One is named Beautiful. The other is still looking for a Name.

④ actions

Faith to see we're KNOWN—(Acts 3:4):

Peter looked straight at the man

Peter said, "Look at us!

The man gave them his attention

Foundation to see we're NAMED and CLAIMED—(Acts 3:6–8):

> Peter says: "In the name of Jesus Christ of Nazareth, walk"

> Peter helps the man rise; he is "fully developed," healed

> The man is healed; runs through the temple gates

5 *outcome*

We're SEEN, KNOWN, NAMED—and claimed—by Jesus. We're made beautiful in Him.

④ *actions*   *What if the God we didn't know, already knows us? What builds the FOUNDATION of our faith?*

ACTIONS [faith to see we're KNOWN]— **(Acts 3:4)**

- *[Peter] looked straight at [the man]*

- *[Peter] said, "Look at us!*

- *[The man] gave them his attention*

ACTIONS [foundation to see we're NAMED and CLAIMED]— **(Acts 3:6–8)**

- *[Peter] says: "In the name of Jesus Christ of Nazareth, walk"*

- *[Peter] helps [the man] rise; is "fully developed," healed*

- *[The man] is healed; runs through temple gates*

⑤ *outcome* ─────────────────

We're SEEN, KNOWN, NAMED—and claimed—by Jesus. We're made beautiful in Him.

① *verse* ACTS 3:2, 4–6 (NIV)

Now a man who was lame from birth was being carried to the temple gate called Beautiful. . . . Peter looked straight at him, as did John. Then Peter said, "Look at us!" So the man gave them his attention, expecting to get something from them. Then Peter said, "Silver or gold I do not have, but what I do have I give to you. In the name of Jesus Christ of Nazareth, walk."

② *design* ——————— *develop* ③

- **NKJV:** *"And <u>fixing his eyes</u> on him, with John, Peter said, '<u>Look at us</u>.' So he <u>gave them his attention</u>, expecting to receive something from them."*

- **LOOK**—*blepó (S. 991):*

  "to look, see, or discern"

  Word choice suggests: "to see something physical with the eyes and find spiritual results from it"

- **BEAUTIFUL**—*hóraios (S. 5611):*

  "fair or beautiful" and "blooming"

  Used figuratively: something has developed and become beautiful in an appointed season of time . . . or something is fruitful because it's fully developed

▶▶ From the Video ◀◀

I have a favorite coffee shop in our small town. It's my unofficial office away from home. I go there to write because the coffee is amazing. The crew is friendly. And the vibe is vintage all over, with classic tunes on the radio, re-claimed wood counters and pipe shelves, and old '60s and '70s vinyl records arranged as art on the wall. There's even the eclectic touch of kayaks in all corners. Sometimes they're out on the river, being used by the shop owner's family, but usually they hang on the wall, tucking me in to my favorite writing table hidden in the back. Everyone seems to know I write at "the coffee shop with kayaks."

Word has gotten out about this coffee shop, and the ladies from our church had a small group that would meet there on Friday mornings. I've even watched from my little table in the back as my mom came in with these ladies, and they owned one corner of the shop for a while. The kind of welcome that I feel when I step into this shop is rare, and it is beautiful. And to be honest, I've gotten used to it after a while. But as I sat in this favorite shop of mine one morning, I never expected to find that I could also be known by GOD in such a personal way.

FEAST TABLE: DISCUSSION

Take a few moments with your group to discuss the video you just watched and explore these concepts in Scripture.

1. Think about the contrast between a temple gate called *Beautiful* and the presence of a broken body and unseen soul, side by side. How do the disciples ensure this man is seen, and known, by God? How are we seen, and known, by Him?

_____

_____

_____

2. Select a volunteer to read Acts 3:8–13 aloud to the group. Why was it important for Peter to tell the crowd that the man's healing came not from their own power but from God's? How is the story of the man's brokenness—and his healing—used to bring others to faith? How can our stories of brokenness and healing encourage the faith of others?

---

3. Luke uses the Greek word *blepó* when Peter tells the lame man to "look at us." If the word choice suggests to see something with our physical eyes and expect spiritual results from it, how much did the man's healing hinge on his decision to first look up? Is healing dependent on our faith?

---

4. Think about the names of God. How important is it for someone to know you enough to call you by name?

Define "beautiful." What makes something fit this definition?

FEAST TABLE: GROUP ACTIVITY

For this activity, each participant will need a Bible, pens/markers, and a smart device (such as a phone or tablet).

- Using a Bible or Bible app on a smart device, look up two additional translations of Acts 3:2, or 3:4–5, and record them on the completed map on pages 44–45.

- To continue your verse mapping journey, pray as a group and <u>select one verse you'll map from Acts 3–6 in individual study time this week.</u> Gather in Week 3 and discuss how your map is the same or differed from others' maps.

FEAST TABLE: CLOSING PRAYER

Let us see the unseen. Let our hearts open to the unknown. Let our prayers be called beautiful to God. Our physical eyes may discern the world around us, but today we pray that our spiritual eyes are the ones that would be opened—make them ready for Your use.

Let our hearts open to the unknown. Let our prayers be called beautiful to God.

INDIVIDUAL STUDY

The Unseen

Now a man who was lame from birth was being carried to the temple gate called Beautiful. . . . Peter looked straight at him, as did John. Then Peter said, "Look at us!" So the man gave them his attention, expecting to get something from them. Then Peter said, "Silver or gold I do not have, but what I do have I give to you. In the name of Jesus Christ of Nazareth, walk."

ACTS 3:2, 4–6

What is beautiful?

This is beautiful. Being named. And known. And seen beyond anything you've known before—so get used to it.

This is faith on fire . . . and it's yours.

In every story of the overlooked, unseen, unknown, and passed by—God delivers the opposite.

FEAST: INDIVIDUAL STUDY INVITATION

You are named. You're seen. No matter what gate you've been frequenting. And here, in this study, you've been called to discover who you are in Him—mapping the life-or-death growth of the early church in Acts 3–6.

This week, you'll encounter boldness—over and over again–in the inspired preaching of apostles (3:11–18). See them remain steadfast against opposition (4:1–4), speak truth even when it feels dangerous or out of their depth (4:5–12) because the Holy Spirit is guiding their tongues. You'll watch as their "learning curve" begins to feel less steep, and you'll absorb confidence with each syllable of truth you map.

Schedule demands, a lack of time, the call of responsibilities, or even thinking we're insignificant to God . . . these things can work to keep our spiritual eyes closed. But going from broken to healed starts by looking up, and realizing who Jesus truly is. And we find Him by spending daily time in the Word.

Read
ACTS 3 — 6

Take time this week, whether five minutes today or an hour tomorrow, to live out that prayer. And see what happens next. See how the BREATH of WIND and the TONGUES of FIRE empower you to dive into God's Word.

Pray and invite the Holy Spirit into your time in the Word. When you are ready, turn to one of the blank verse maps in this section.

Read Acts 3–6. Select and map a verse that speaks to your heart. If your group selected a verse to map and discuss together, map that verse this week as well. Prepare to discuss what you've learned when your group gathers again.

Once we're gathered around the feast table, we might be surprised at how KNOWN we already are, right WHERE we are.

Study Prompt

What gets lost in translation? How do the different translations present the same ideas or biblical principles?

The *design* identifies what the verse is calling attention to by comparing translations. The *design* calls out similar word choice, repetition of words, phrases, and/or aspects of grammar common across multiple translations. It brings to light what the verse is saying that cannot be lost to translation, and what may stand out as translation specific. Anything here could trigger a question or path for further investigation.

Study Support Examples

Information you might find in your research . . .

Acts 4:25–28 Psalm 2 describes the surrounding nations rebelling against the Davidic king. God enthrones and vindicates his anointed one, warning these nations against rebellion. The believers apply the psalm to the actions of King Herod, Pontius Pilate, the Gentiles (Roman soldiers), and "the people of Israel" (the religious leaders) against Jesus, God's Anointed One (cf. Luke 23). Their evil actions turned out to be exactly what God's "power and will had decided before-hand should happen." Though God did not will their evil actions, his plan all along was to use their evil actions to accomplish his salvation.

4:25 You [God] spoke by the Holy Spirit through the mouth of . . . David. A remarkable statement expressing the nature of biblical inspiration.

4:29 The apostles pray not for safety but "to speak your word with great boldness."

Model of the semicircular Nicanor Gate, a possible location for the "Beautiful" gate where the lame man was placed to beg (Acts 3:2).

4  actions

What actions develop the story in this verse? What is happening in this verse? To whom?

5 outcome _____

What is God saying to me today? How do I apply this to my life?

1 *verse*   What verse am I mapping? What key themes or specific words are speaking to me today?

2 *design* ——————————— *develop* **3**

What different translations make up the design for this verse? Underline key phrases or words repeated.

What is the Hebrew or Greek meaning for the underlined phrases or words?

4  What actions develop the story in this verse? What is happening in this verse? To whom?

5 *outcome*

What is God saying to me today? How do I apply this to my life?

1 *verse*

What verse am I mapping? What key themes or specific words are speaking to me today?

2 *design* ———————— *develop* **3**

What different translations make up the design for this verse? Underline key phrases or words repeated.

What is the Hebrew or Greek meaning for the underlined phrases or words?

session
3

Made to Stand

But Stephen, full of the Holy Spirit, looked up to heaven and saw the glory of God, and Jesus standing at the right hand of God.

ACTS 7:55

What fears could possibly stand against us when our Savior stands for us?

OPENING REFLECTION

When we enter a fight we can't win on our own, it can become a crisis point for our faith. But in this story, we find Jesus' promise that He'll never leave us when we go into battle. Jesus will stand against every storm, and He'll bridge the gap between our faith and embracing His faithfulness every time.

What if our fears of losing comfort, safety, and earthly securities threaten to stand in the way of fully surrendering to Jesus? Watch and see. When we battle for our faith, eternity takes notice.

Our fears can't stand against us when the Savior of the world stands for us.

FEASTING AND GETTING STARTED

Welcome back to session three of *Acts: Feasting on the Abundance of God's Word.*

We've gathered for a third time—by now beginning to feast on the Word, and leaning on our Savior in spaces we may not have considered before. Our confidence has begun to grow in our study time. We find our confidence assured that the Holy Spirit will continue to meet us where we are, and stand with us as we continue to learn.

As we gather to feast this week, discuss the following in group share:

- *Compare and contrast the verse your group mapped. What did you discover through mapping the group verse? Where did your exploration take you?*

- *How did the Holy Spirit make you aware that you're seen, and uniquely known, by Him this week? Did He meet you where you were in your individual study time?*

FEASTING: VIDEO STORY

Play the video segment for session three. As you watch the next installment of our book of Acts story, follow the verse mapping guide points starting on the next page and refer to the completed map on pages 62–63. Take brief notes or record questions that might lead you to further research in your independent study time this week.

Crossroads of faith are scary.

Notes

① *verse*

What stands out in these verses:

When we face loss, "How do I find You?" and "How do I accept this?" become our questions to God. His response—patient, loving, immediate—is to make us whole.

While we may not be able to change what's happening in our TODAY, God is already working to fix our TOMORROWS

Surrendering to Christ doesn't eliminate opposition or persecution in our lives, but when we stand *for* Him, He stands *with* us

In the New International Version, the ONLY TIME the Bible references Jesus STANDING at God's right hand is in back-to-back verses at the stoning of Stephen . . . the first recorded martyr's death for faith in Jesus Christ (Acts 7:55–56)

② *design*

New International Version: Stephen is "full of the Holy Spirit" as he "looked up to heaven and saw the glory of God, and Jesus standing at the right hand of God"

New King James Version: Uses similar language, telling us Stephen is "full of the Holy Spirit" as he "gazed into heaven, and saw the glory of God, and Jesus standing at the right hand of God." (Two times, Luke tells us.)

Other translations: the mob is rioting around Stephen, yet "he hardly noticed—he only had eyes for God" (MSG), and "he gazed intently into heaven" (NASB). Stephen proclaims, "Oh! I see heaven wide open and the Son of Man standing at God's side!" (MSG), and, "Behold, I see the heavens opened up and the Son of Man standing at the right hand of God" (NASB).

The "he only had eyes for God" statement is powerful—it models how we focus on heaven here on earth, by locking our eyes on Jesus. When He's all we want to have, He'll be all we see.

③ develop

In the Greek, *plérés* (S. 4134) means "abounding in; complete, or completely occupied with." Used as an adjective, it denotes a "full life."

In the Greek, *atenizó* (S. 816) means "to direct my gaze; look steadily." The word comes from the Greek *teinō*, adding the meaning "to stretch, or strain." Stephen isn't just looking up at the sky. He's kneeling (Acts 7:60), and would have to stretch or strain to look up and keep such focused attention on Christ.

④ actions

Stephen OBEYS—fixes his eyes on God and directs his intent focus on eternity, rather than what is earthly:

Is "full of faith and of the Holy Spirit" (Acts 6:5)

"Performed great wonders and signs among the people" (Acts 6:8)

Delivers a scathing rebuke against Sanhedrin—for unbelief and responsibility for killing God's Son (Acts 7:1–53)

The Holy Spirit gave Stephen the wisdom to speak (Acts 6:10)

⑤ outcome

When we stand for Jesus through our FEARS, He stands for us. If we obey and fix our eyes on Him—even unto dying to ourselves—there's nothing that can stand against us.

But Stpehen, full of the Holy Spirit, hardly noticed—he only had eyes for God.
ACTS 7:55 (MSG)

SESSION 3

④ *actions* **What fears could possibly stand against, when our Savior stands for us?**

Stephen OBEYS—fixes his eyes on God; directs his intent focus on eternity, rather than what is earthly:

- *Is ". . . full of faith and of the Holy Spirit"* (**Acts 6:5**)

- *". . . performed great wonders and signs among the people"* (**Acts 6:8**)

- *. . . delivers a scathing rebuke against Sanhedrin—for unbelief and responsibility for killing God's Son* (**Acts 7:1–53**)

- *Holy Spirit . . . gave Stephen the wisdom to speak* (**Acts 6:10**)

Only ONCE in the Bible does Jesus stand "at the right hand of God" (**Acts 7:55**)

⑤ *outcome* ———————————————————

When we stand for Jesus through our FEARS, He stands for us. If we obey and fix our eyes on Him—even unto dying to ourselves—there's nothing that can stand against us.

1 verse   **ACTS 7:55 (NIV)**

But Stephen, full of the Holy Spirit, looked up to heaven and saw the glory of God, and Jesus standing at the right hand of God . . .

2 design ———————— **develop 3**

- **NKJV:** *"But he, being <u>full of the Holy Spirit, gazed</u> into heaven and saw the glory of God, and <u>Jesus standing</u> at the right hand of God . . ."*

- **FULL**—*plérés (S. 4134):*

  "abounding in; complete," or "completely occupied with"

  Used as an adjective to denote a "full life"

- **LOOKED**—*atenizó (S. 816):*

  "to direct my gaze; look steadily"

  Comes from the Greek *teinō*: meaning "to stretch, or strain"

  Used as an adjective to denote a "full life"

From the Video

I'd dreamed about being a Christian author for more than a decade. Our close-knit family had stepped out on the road together—celebrating the highs, cheerleading through the lows, and encouraging me to keep going during two years of rejections. Then, one Friday in May, we finally got a "yes." The dream was happening! I had a publishing family, and I was going to be a Christian author. Everything we'd worked for, prayed over, and walked toward was about to happen. The call I'd felt on my heart to step out and dream-chase with God suddenly became real.

I didn't think anything could faze our joy on that day. But an hour later, I got a call from my dad. He said, "This could be bad. I may have leukemia." Before I knew it, our family had embarked on an author-and-cancer journey, walking the super-high highs of this dream that had come true while valley-walking through the super-low lows of a rare and aggressive form of leukemia. It was five months of wonderful and terrible, packaged side by side.

FEAST TABLE: GROUP DISCUSSION

Take a few moments with your group to discuss the video you just watched and explore these concepts in Scripture.

1. Think about the areas of our lives in which we have relative safety, comfort, and security. Regardless of the threats to these things in their earthly life, the disciples instead chose to focus on eternity—even rejoicing that they were called worthy to suffer for Christ's name (Acts 5:41). Is it possible to rejoice in times of suffering? Discuss how our witness is strengthened if we can rejoice in the midst of suffering.

2. Select a volunteer to read Acts 6:8–10 aloud to the group. Stephen lived a life of integrity, full of "faith and power," yet he did not escape opposition or persecution for his faith. Is persecution something every believer must be willing to accept in order to follow Christ? How does the Holy Spirit enable us to withstand persecution?

_____

_____

_____

3. How does wholeness transcend what we're going through *today* in order to prepare us for *tomorrow*?

_____

_____

_____

4. What effect might it have had on Saul (later, to become the apostle Paul) to have been instrumental in and witness Stephen's execution?

_____

_____

_____

Define "whole." What does wholeness look like in the life of a believer?

_____

_____

_____

SESSION 3

As a group, look up and read the Scripture references where Jesus is SEATED or SAT DOWN at God's right hand (Matthew 22:44; 26:64; Mark 12:36; 14:62; 16:19; Luke 20:42; 22:69; Acts 2:34; Ephesians 1:20; Colossians 3:1; Hebrews 1:3; 8:1; 10:12; 12:12) or where Jesus is exalted, and making intercession at God's right hand (Acts 2:25; 2:33; 5:31; Romans 8:34; Hebrews 1:13; 1 Peter 3:22). Then discuss why Stephen's death is the only reference we have of Jesus STANDING at God's right hand.

FEAST TABLE: GROUP ACTIVITY

For this activity, you will need a Bible, pens/markers, and a smart device (such as a phone or tablet).

- Using a Bible or Bible app on a smart device, look up two additional translations of Acts 7:55, and record them on the completed map on pages 62–63.

- To continue your verse mapping journey, pray as a group and select one verse you'll map from Acts 7–8 in individual study time this week. Gather in Week 4 and discuss how your map is the same or differed from others' maps.

FEAST TABLE: CLOSING PRAYER

No fear can stand against us when our Savior stands for us. As we stand for Christ, as we obey, and fix our eyes on Him—even unto dying to ourselves—we pray and believe there's nothing that can stand against us.

No fear can stand against us when our Savior stands for us.

INDIVIDUAL STUDY

Made to Stand

But Stephen, full of the Holy Spirit, looked up to heaven and saw the glory of God, and Jesus standing at the right hand of God.

ACTS 7:55

Jesus is an active participant when we stand for Him. We can be assured that whatever opposition or persecution we withstand in the earthly life creates a new, closer-to-whole version of ourselves in the eternal one. When we serve, toil, and even battle for our faith, eternity stands up and takes notice.

FEAST: INDIVIDUAL STUDY INVITATION

Jesus stands for YOU.

Think about that. It's a personal moment, His eyes fixed on you. So engaged in your story that He's drawn to move in closer. To rise up. To show His recognition of your study and sacrifice and surrender.

When you seek . . . when you go deeper . . . when you're willing to give up everything for Him, He refuses to sit in passivity. But He's also there through your times of rebellion (Acts 7:37–43) and resistance (7:51–53). And certainly through persecution (7:55–56). Even by those who doubt but will one day experience the moment of life-change when Christ stands in their presence (8:1–3). He stays intimately involved in the details of your journey.

Read
A C T S 7 — 8

Pray just before you go through these chapters. Whether it's five minutes today or an hour tomorrow, invite the Holy Spirit and gather with Him.

Read Acts 7–8. Focus on the wholeness God offers us past this earthly life. Our opportunity is to fix our eyes on Jesus as He stands for us. Explore. Engage. Endeavor to go so far with your faith in Him . . . that He's forced out of his chair. Every chapter of your story is laid bare at His feet. And while Stephen's martyrdom may have been the first time He stood at the Father's right hand, it won't be the last.

Study Prompt

Actions record:

- What's happening in the verse

- Who the characters are in what you're reading

- How their story relates to other stories/verses/persons in other areas of Scripture

- What are the topics, themes, dates of significant events, and/or theological elements of the verse(s) you're researching

Study Support Examples

Information you might find in your research . . .

III. The Witness Beyond Jerusalem (6:1–12:24)

  A. The Choosing of the Seven (6:1–7)

  B. Stephen's Arrest and Martyrdom (6:8–7:60)

    1. Stephen Seized (6:8–15)

    2. Stephen's Speech to the Sanhedrin (7:1–53)

    3. The Stoning of Stephen (7:54–60)

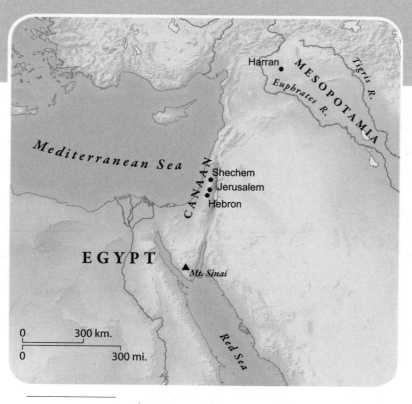

Many of the places mentioned in Stephen's speech

Excerpted from *NIV Biblical Theology Study Bible*. Copyright © 2015, 2018, Zondervan.

4 *actions* What actions develop the story in this verse? What is happening in this verse? To whom?

5 *outcome* What is God saying to me today? How do I apply this to my life?

1 *verse* — What verse am I mapping? What key themes or specific words are speaking to me today?

2 *design* ——————————— *develop* 3

What different translations make up the design for this verse? Underline key phrases or words repeated.

What is the Hebrew or Greek meaning for the underlined phrases or words?

④ *actions* What actions develop the story in this verse? What is happening in this verse? To whom?

⑤ *outcome* What is God saying to me today? How do I apply this to my life?

1 *verse* What verse am I mapping? What key themes or specific words are speaking to me today?

2 *design* ——————————— *develop* **3**

What different translations make up the design for this verse? Underline key phrases or words repeated.

What is the Hebrew or Greek meaning for the underlined phrases or words?

Broken

After taking some food, he regained his strength.
Saul spent several days with the disciples in Damascus. At once
he began to preach in the synagogues that Jesus is the Son of
God. . . . Yet Saul grew more and more powerful and baffled the
Jews living in Damascus by proving that Jesus is the Messiah.

ACTS 9:19–22

This is the story of a zealot's quest. A road of brokenness and strength. And a Savior who's about to restore the view . . . because "broken" is actually where a new story road begins.

OPENING REFLECTION

It's not easy to see clearly through times of brokenness. Our sight can be stunted by pain, doubt, fears, and the outcome of our FAILURES. When we can't see our way out of a mess, the things we *can* see can begin to look like a safe place to hide. But in Acts 9, we see clearly how our FAILURES . . . our brokenness . . . aren't where the story ends.

In Acts 10–16 we find a murderer. A zealout. A sinner with shattered arrogance. A scholar who's taken back to school on who Jesus is . . . and all of this is in the DNA of the same man. Saul. Who receives new sight (9:17–18), new zeal (9:20–22), a new mission (9:15–16), and even a new name (13:9)—all out of brokenness.

You'll witness it all in detail—how you too can have an encounter with Jesus so life-altering that you never get over it. And the former brokenness doesn't matter as much anymore; now that you've tasted redemption, He's all that matters.

What if our faithlessness to God could not impact His faithfulness to us?

FEASTING AND GETTING STARTED

Welcome back to session four of *Acts: Feasting on the Abundance of God's Word.*

We've gathered for week four—having already seen how the Holy Spirit was faithful in building the FOUNDATION and FAITH of the new church, and helped its early followers to overcome FEAR that could have stunted their journey. This week, we gather to discuss brokenness, and the restoration that makes our FAILURES a thing of the past.

As we gather to feast this week, discuss the following in group share:

- *Compare and contrast the verse your group mapped. What did you discover through mapping the group verse?*

- *What verse(s) did you select to map, and why?*

- *What moments of faith-building did you experience in self-study time this week? Was there opposition when making that intentional effort to spend time with God? Were you able to lean on Christ to stand as your defender in those moments?*

FEASTING: VIDEO STORY

Play the video segment for session four. As you watch the next installment of our book of Acts story, follow the verse mapping guide points starting on the next page and refer to the completed map on pages 80–81. Take brief notes or record questions that might lead you to further research in your independent study time this week.

Notes

1 verse

What stands out in these verses:

> Our vision of God's plan can be stunted by pain, doubt, fears, and the outcome of our FAILURES. But it's in our brokenness—past, present, and future—that we see Christ has already marked us for redemption.

> Relying on our own strength to fix what's been broken will be surpassed by His grace every time

> The Holy Spirit doesn't wait to enable us to speak boldly (Acts 9:20)—we're restored, strengthened, and then we go

2 design

> The NIV: "After taking some food, he regained his strength"—Saul begins to preach in the synagogues that Jesus is the Son of God.

> Other translations echo the same strength-growth (NKJV, NASB) for Saul—who will soon become known throughout the rest of Acts as Paul (Acts 13:9).

> Paul "was strengthened" and "got to his feet, was baptized, and sat down with them to a hearty meal" (MSG).

SESSION 4

The strengthening in both Paul's body and spirit results in his restoration. He is filled with the Holy Spirit (Acts 9:17). Paul's "momentum was up now and he plowed straight into the opposition, disarming the Damascus Jews and trying to show them that this Jesus was the Messiah" (Acts 9:22 MSG).

③ develop

In the Greek, *enischuó* (S. 1765) means "to invigorate, or strengthen." The use of this word is intensified to "engaging, assaulting strength"—meaning Paul has been given strength enough to face confrontation.

In the Greek, *endunamoó* (S. 1743) means "filled with power; strengthened." The use of this word in the phrase "more and more powerful" is intensified to mean the ability to share this strength with others—Paul is being empowered to impart his spiritual strength to other believers.

④ actions

Saul [Paul] is strengthened in FAILURE (and brokenness):

Physical strength is restored, enabling him to begin to preach (Acts 9:19)

Spiritual strength—his momentum and power—enables him to plow through opposition (Acts 9:22)

Spiritual strength results in courage that enables him to flee Damascus following a threat and continue to preach (Acts 9:25)

Fortitude that enables him to withstand the rejection of the disciples (Acts 9:26) and fearlessness that enables him to speak boldly in the name of the Lord

5 outcome

Our moments of FAILURE + the STRENGTH and fortitude of God = our RESTORATION. He can grow our spiritual strength from the broken places.

Moments of brokenness force us to look to God.

4 actions

What if our faithlessness to God could not impact His faithfulness to us?

Saul [Paul] is strengthened in FAILURE [and brokenness]:

- *Physical strength is restored, enabling him to begin to preach* **(Acts 9:19)**

- *Spiritual strength—his momentum and power—enables him to plow through opposition* **(Acts 9:22)**

- *Spiritual strength results in courage that enables him to flee Damascus following a threat and continue to preach* **(Acts 9:25)**

- *Fortitude that enables him to withstand the rejection of the disciples* **(Acts 9:26)** *and fearlessness that enables him to speak boldly in the name of the Lord*

Before, Saul had been zealous—Paul found true strength in his brokenness.

5 outcome

Our moments of FAILURE + the STRENGTH and fortitude of God = our RESTORATION. He can grow our spiritual strength from the broken places.

① *verse* — ACTS 9:19–22 (NIV)

After taking some food, he regained his strength. Saul spent several days with the disciples in Damascus. At once he began to preach in the synagogues that Jesus is the Son of God. . . . Yet Saul grew more and more powerful and baffled the Jews living in Damascus by proving that Jesus is the Messiah.

② *design* ——————————— *develop* ③

- **NKJV:** *"But Saul <u>increased all the more in strength</u>, and confounded the Jews who dwelt in Damascus by proving that this Jesus is the Christ."*

- **STRENGTH (v. 19)**—*enischuó* (S. 1765):

  "to invigorate, or strengthen"

  Use of word intensified to: "engaging, assaulting strength" [Saul given strength enough to face confrontation]

- **STRENGTH (v. 22)**—*endunamoó* (S. 1743):

  "filled with power; strengthened"

  Use of word intensified to: "more and more powerful"; Saul given ability to share this strength with others

▶ *From the Video* ◀

It was one of those defining moments—an opportunity I knew wasn't going to come around again. I'd been presented with a potential dream job.

If I wanted to, I could go back to the security I knew in my corporate career. I was being offered the do-over of a lifetime—to work for a company I'd dreamed about for years. I could make more in salary than I'd ever made before. I could move cross-country to a state where I already had family. I could travel the world, write, and design for a major corporation . . . all the things I loved. It was not just A job—it was THE job I'd always wanted. And it stirred the creative side of my soul like few things could.

The only catch? It was a full-focus commitment. There would be no time for the ministry calling burning on my heart, or writing for Jesus on the side. It came down to a decision: I could say yes to my dream, or, without any guarantees, I could once say yes to God.

FEAST TABLE: DISCUSSION

Take a few moments with your group to discuss the story you just watched and explore these concepts in Scripture.

1. Think about the dramatic shift between Saul's zealous persecution of Christians before encountering Christ on the road to Damascus and the complete change of his heart after. Where were the moments of forgiveness that affected his heart-change, and how did they work to strengthen the call God had placed on his life? What outcomes can we expect when we're "filled with the Holy Spirit" (Acts 9:17)?

2. Select a volunteer (or more than one) to read Acts 2:1–15, 4:8–13, and 4:29–31 aloud to the group. Just as with Saul's experience on the road to Damascus, how does the Holy Spirit enable us to gain strength and speak boldly—even out of brokenness?

_____

_____

3. How can past failures—and fears of future ones—cause spiritual "blind spots" in our faith? How was the restoration of Saul's physical sight symbolic of what had occurred with his spiritual sight?

_____

_____

4. The course of Saul's story road changed when Christ gave him a new story, on an unexpected road. How can God use the "unexpected" on our story roads to bless and encourage others on theirs?

_____

_____

Define "broken." What does brokenness look like?

_____

_____

Think back to a time of brokenness in your own life. If it resulted from your fears or failures, how might Christ redeem and heal those scarred places?

FEAST TABLE: GROUP ACTIVITY

For this activity, you will need a Bible, pens/markers, and a smart device (such as a phone or tablet).

- Using a Bible or Bible app on a smart device, look up two additional translations of Acts 9:19–22, and record them on the completed map on pages 80–81.

- To continue your verse mapping journey, pray as a group and select one verse you'll map from Acts 10–16 in individual study time this week. Gather in Week 5 and discuss how your map is the same or differed from others' maps.

FEAST TABLE: CLOSING PRAYER

When we step out on a new story road with God, we can't always avoid brokenness. We pray that when we encounter moments that break us down, we'll look to Christ for our building up. Instead of relying on our own strength to save ourselves, we recognize where our true strength rests, and that our failures don't define us; Jesus does.

Our failures don't define us;
Jesus does.

session 4

INDIVIDUAL STUDY

After taking some food, he regained his strength.
Saul spent several days with the disciples in Damascus. At once
he began to preach in the synagogues that Jesus is the Son of
God. . . . Yet Saul grew more and more powerful and baffled the
Jews living in Damascus by proving that Jesus is the Messiah.

ACTS 9:19–22

FAILURE + STRENGTH and Fortitude of God = RESTORATION.

God's faithfulness endures, and He can take our failures, brokenness, and wobbly-faith moments to strengthen us in a way we never thought possible. He can grow our spiritual strength in the broken places as we study the Word for the future times when we need to apply it to our lives.

FEAST: INDIVIDUAL STUDY INVITATION

See what happens next as the once-broken Saul becomes the redeemed and restored Paul. And as you do, look for God to lead us to redemption for the spiritual blind spots we may not have known we have.

Let's open our eyes.

SESSION 4

Read

ACTS 10 – 16

Pray and determine where you'll spend time with the Holy Spirit in Acts 10–16. If your heart needs building up after the process of breaking down, go back and research verses that confirm Jesus provides strength and grace in the midst of our brokenness: Acts 9:17–18 or 9:26–30.

Read Acts 10–16. Reflect. Relive and explore wherever you need to. In your past. With new sight. Revived zeal. With a new mission to research the times when mere men are filled with the Holy Spirit (9:17; 13:9; 13:52), and what the outcomes are. If your group selected a verse that you'd like to read and discuss together, then map that verse and prepare to discuss what you've learned when your group gathers again.

This is your fate . . . to be broken no more.

Study Prompt

The outcome is a quick-hit summary of what you've learned. One or two sentences should do it. Summarize, jot it down, and come back later to find where the Holy Spirit has confirmed His promises to you. This is your claim on this verse, at this time of your life. The outcome should reflect whatever truth has been revealed in your map.

The Spirit's strength is found in the wobbly faith moments.

Study Support Examples

Information you might find in your research . . .

The Holy Spirit as guide, empowering agent, and sign of the new age. For Luke, the gift of the Holy Spirit marks the dawn of the new age of salvation that Jesus' life, death, and resurrection inaugurate. The book has often been called the "Acts of the Holy Spirit" because the Spirit plays a leading role. During Jesus' public ministry he alone is endowed with the Spirit and performs miracles and exorcisms in the power of the Holy Spirit. In Acts, by virture of his death, resurrection, and exaltation to the right hand of God, Jesus pours out the Spirit, empowering his disciples for mission (2:1–24:33; see Joel 2:28–32). Throughout the rest of Acts, the Spirit fills and empowers believers (2:4; 4:8, 31; 6:3, 5; 7:55; 9:17; 11:24) and guides and directs the progress of the gospel (8:29, 39; 10:19–20; 11:28; 13:2, 9–12; 16:6–7; 21:4).

Paul's first missionary journey ca. AD 46–47 (Acts 12:25–14:28)

4 *actions*

What actions develop the story in this verse? What is happening in this verse? To whom?

5 *outcome*

What is God saying to me today? How do I apply this to my life?

1 *verse* What verse am I mapping? What key themes or specific words are speaking to me today?

2 *design* ──────── *develop* **3**

What different translations make up the design for this verse? Underline key phrases or words repeated.

What is the Hebrew or Greek meaning for the underlined phrases or words?

4 *actions*

What actions develop the story in this verse? What is happening in this verse? To whom?

5 *outcome*

What is God saying to me today? How do I apply this to my life?

1 *verse*   What verse am I mapping? What key themes or specific words are speaking to me today?

2 *design* —————————————— *develop* **3**

What different translations make up the design for this verse? Underline key phrases or words repeated.

What is the Hebrew or Greek meaning for the underlined phrases or words?

session 5

The Saved

So Peter was kept in prison, but the church was earnestly praying to God for him. The night before Herod was to bring him to trial, Peter was sleeping. . . . Suddenly an angel of the Lord appeared. . . . "Quick, get up!" he said, and the chains fell off Peter's wrists.

ACTS 12:5–7

What if God was only as far away as we're willing to turn toward Him?

OPENING REFLECTION

On the mission field of our faith, how far will God go to pursue us?

    This week we enter into a seemingly impossible situation for Peter: he's thrown into a Roman prison, chained at the wrists, tethered to soldiers, awaiting the fate of execution the following day. Circumstances are dark, and hope is bleak. Until we look closer. We see God's intervention in a miraculous way—both through Peter's absolute trust, and the faith and hope of the early church.

    We see peace in the midst of chaos. Rest in the center of turmoil. Faith and prayer . . . and God's immediate response in the zealous pursuit of one of His own.

FEASTING AND GETTING STARTED

Welcome back to session five of *Acts: Feasting on the Abundance of God's Word.*

The foundation of our faith has been anchored. Fears and failures are behind us. And as we gather to feast on the Word this week, we see how valued we are by the pursuit of our God. Discuss the following to prepare your heart during group share:

- *Compare and contrast the verse your group mapped. What did you discover through mapping the group verse?*

- *What verse(s) did you select to map, and why? How did it go?*

- *What past failures or present fears did the Holy Spirit bring to light during study time this week? Where were you strengthened? How did the Holy Spirit fill you with boldness in your faith-walk?*

FEASTING: VIDEO STORY

Play the video segment for session five. As you watch the next installment of our book of Acts story, follow the verse mapping guide points starting on the next page and refer to the completed map on pages 98–99. Take brief notes or record questions that might lead you to further research in your independent study time this week.

Can you imagine a life without Jesus?

Notes

 ① verse

What stands out in these verses:

> In a devastating loss for the early church, King Herod Agrippa—the ruler over Judea—has just put to death James, one of Jesus's closest disciples. Bolstered by public approval, he imprisons Peter for the same eventual fate. But his actions are halted by Jewish law, which prevents executions during the Feast of Unleavened Bread (Passover week).

> God will go to the depths of our impossible circumstances—and to the borders of our faith—in order to pursue us

> Despite our spiritual growth (like the growth of the early church), there still remains a threat of opposition and persecution in the lives of believers. Faithful prayer is a catalyst for God to respond with swift action.

② design

> "Peter was sleeping" in the NKJV, and "Peter slept like a baby" in the Message. He's also "bound with two chains between two soldiers; and the guards before the door were keeping the prison" (NKJV).

> In the New International Version, several phrases that stand out—for Peter, for the believers in Jerusalem, and for God—starting with, "the church was earnestly praying to God for him."

New King James Version: Peter was in prison awaiting execution, "but constant prayer was offered to God for him by the church."

Other translations: "All the time that Peter was under heavy guard in the jailhouse, the church prayed for him most strenuously" (MSG), and, "But prayer for him was being made fervently by the church to God" (NASB).

③ *develop*

In the Greek, *ektenós* (S. 1619) means "fervently or strenuously; without slack; or without undue letup." The same word is used to describe Jesus' fervent prayer in the garden before His crucifixion (Luke 22:44)

In the Greek, *koimaó* (S. 2837) means "to put to sleep or fall asleep." The word means to be in such deep sleep, it's sometimes likened to the eternal rest of death.

④ *actions* to show God's pursuit

Peter trusts God so completely, he is able to sleep (Acts 12:6)

The church prays—earnestly expecting God's deliverance (Acts 12:5)

God responds—sends an angel to break the chains and deliver Peter from impossible circumstances (Acts 12:7)

Peter goes from sleeping to saved, chained to free, and alone to escorted out of the pit with an angel of light leading the way

5 *outcome*

Prayer and faith are important weapons in the life of a believer. God uses both to deliver us from impossible circumstances, and pursues us—especially when we've been far away.

Faithful prayer is a catalyst for God to respond with swift action.

4

What if God was only as far away as we're willing to turn toward Him? How far will He go to pursue us?

ACTIONS to show God's pursuit:

- *Peter is trusting—able to sleep* (Acts 12:6)

- *The people are praying—earnestly expecting God's deliverance* (Acts 12:5)

- *God is responding—sends an angel to break the chains; delivers Peter from impossible circumstances* (Acts 12:7)

Peter goes from sleeping to SAVED. Chained to FREE. And alone to ESCORTED out of the pit with an angel of light leading the way.

5 outcome

Prayer and faith are important weapons in the life of a believer. God uses both to deliver us from impossible circumstances, and pursues us—especially when we've been far away.

1 *verse*   **ACTS 12:5–7 (NIV)**

So Peter was kept in prison, but the church was <u>earnestly praying</u> to God for him. The night before Herod was to bring him to trial, Peter was sleeping. . . . Suddenly an angel of the Lord appeared. . . . "Quick, get up!" he said, and the chains fell off Peter's wrists.

2 *design* ───────────── *develop* 3

NKJV: *"Peter was therefore kept in prison, but <u>constant prayer</u> was offered to God for him by the church . . . that night Peter was <u>sleeping</u> . . . an angel of the Lord stood by him . . . saying, "Arise quickly!" And his chains fell off his hands.*

- **EARNESTLY [praying]**—*ektenós* (S. 1619):

  "fervently or strenuously; without slack; or without undue letup"

  The SAME WORD used in Luke 22:44 to describe Jesus' fervent prayer in the garden before His crucifixion

- **SLEEP**—*koimaó* (S. 2837):

  "to put to sleep or fall asleep"

  To be in such deep sleep, sometimes likened unto death

▶ *From the Video* ◀

I slipped into my aisle seat and settled in for the two-hour plane ride, all-too ready to go home. Normally, I'd have closed my eyes and slept through it all. But I'd noticed a book peeking out from the seatback pocket of the man sitting next to me. I'll admit—I'm the nosey, bookish type. If I see a book, I go right for asking about it. That was enough to get us talking.

He was a kind man, a generation older than I. Quiet and respectful. He had patient eyes and an easy manner. And I would learn that he was an ardent atheist.

It was quite a stretch for both of us based on the lenses with which we looked at the world. But he didn't cringe when I told him of my life choice to follow Jesus. Instead, he asked questions—each without a debating or critical tone. He listened . . . I answered. And I asked questions of him. He answered . . . I listened. It was everything you don't find in a debate on social media. This was looking back in someone's eyes, trying to imagine what life was like from their view. And honestly . . . I was struggling with it. I couldn't imagine a life without Jesus.

FEAST TABLE: DISCUSSION

Take a few moments with your group to discuss the story you just watched and explore these concepts in Scripture.

1. Think about what conditions were like in a first-century Roman prison. Why is Peter able to rest in the midst of a seemingly hopeless situation, even on the night before his execution? How does God come through in our impossible situations?

---

2. Select a volunteer to read Acts 12:5–15 aloud to the group. Discuss how far God pursues Peter to free him. Is the breaking of chains from Peter's wrists symbolic of the chain-breaking God can do in our lives?

3. Leading up to events in Acts 12, the early church sees explosive growth, spreading to Samaria, Judea, Galilee, and Antioch—where believers are referred to as "Christians" for the very first time (Acts 11:26). How did the faith of the disciples affect the spread of the gospel message? In what ways did they trust God for their protection and provision in order for the church to grow?

4. Despite the devastating loss for the early church with James' execution, the believers did not lose hope when Peter's life was also threatened. Instead, they prayed "fervently and strenuously" through the night, expecting God's deliverance come morning. When instinct tells us all hope is lost, how do we still cling to God's promises that He will deliver us? Have you ever seen your most fervent prayers answered?

Define "hope." What does it look like to cling to hope in a seemingly hopeless situation?

_____

_____

_____

Think back to a time when you could have trusted God but didn't. What was the outcome of the situation? How can you trust Him next time?

_____

_____

_____

FEAST TABLE: GROUP ACTIVITY

For this activity, you will need a Bible, pens/markers, and a smart device (such as a phone or tablet).

- Using a Bible or Bible app on a smart device, look up two additional translations of Acts 12:5–7, and record them on the completed map on pages 98–99.

- To continue your verse mapping journey, pray as a group and select one verse you'll map from Acts 17–20 in individual study time this week. Gather in Week 6 and discuss how your map is the same or differed from others' maps.

FEAST TABLE: CLOSING PRAYER

As the church did for Peter, we pray earnestly—for God's presence, provision, and His ultimate deliverance from the seemingly impossible situations we may face. We trust that as we study the Word and open our hearts to new growth, we can withstand any opposition that comes against our faith in Him.

INDIVIDUAL STUDY

The Saved

So Peter was kept in prison, but the church was earnestly praying to God for him. The night before Herod was to bring him to trial, Peter was sleeping. . . . Suddenly an angel of the Lord appeared. . . . "Quick, get up!" he said, and the chains fell off Peter's wrists.

ACTS 12:5–7

FEAST: INDIVIDUAL STUDY INVITATION

Before this week, you may have seen yourself like Peter. Maybe you've been held behind walls you can't break down on your own. Wondering behind barriers of a lack of confidence, a packed schedule, brokenness, past hurts, and an uncertain future . . . but there's hope. Like the church that refused to cease praying, you've stepped into another week of ceaseless time in the Word. And in these words is the summons to freedom. Because this isn't a final night behind bars; this is a story like Peter's (12:7–10). The invitation for the chain-breaking, door-demolishing deliverance of your life. And to really LIVE. Because prison is for the condemned, and that's not you.

The chains will fall. The walls crumble. For every page you turn in your Bible, you embark on another prison break, and you choose to feast on freedom.

SESSION 5

Past sessions took us on a verse mapping journey through the barriers of FAITH and our FOUNDATION, and the FEARS and FAILURES we may encounter as we walk with Jesus. But this week, think about the freedom that's waiting. Think about where you've been (behind bars), and where you're going. (Here's a hint: The FEAST is coming.) Think about the weapon of prayer we already possess and how God pursues us—no matter how far away we might be.

Read
ACTS 17 — 20

Pray. The beginning of something good can be hit with barriers along the way. Pray for the Holy Spirit's presence and deliverance from the barriers that may seek to stunt the growth in your journey.

Read Acts 17–20. Continue this week to look at the growth of the church, the spread of the gospel of Jesus Christ, and how His disciples continually overcame barriers to authentically walk with God and serve Him with their lives. You'll find the saved fanning out to share their redemption story with the hungry in places called Thessalonica (17:1–4), Athens (17:16–21), Corinth (18:1–8), and eventually Ephesus (19:1–41).

If your group selected a verse that you'd like to read and discuss together, then map that as well and prepare to discuss what you've learned when your group gathers again.

You've been given an open door to freedom, so get ready . . .

Time to break free.

Study Prompt

What verse are you mapping? What key themes or specific words are speaking to you today?

- *What's on your heart today?* If you're facing a difficult circumstance, or find yourself in an unexpected path in your own story with God, select a verse(s) that speaks to the theme of your heart for today.

- *What's that word?* If you're reading Scripture and something jumps off the page—a word you don't recognize, a city you've never heard of, or a phrase you don't quite understand—this is a good indication it might be your verse(s) to map for the day.

Then Peter came to himself and said, "Now I know without a doubt that the Lord has sent his angel and rescued me from Herod's clutches and from everything the Jewish people were hoping would happen."
(ACTS 12:11)

SESSION 5

Study Support Examples

Information you might find in your research . . .

18:1–17 *In Corinth.* From Athens, Paul moves on to Corinth, where he spends 18 months (v. 11), the longest in any church except for Ephesus, where he stayed about three years (19:8, 10). As major cities in the empire, Corinth and Ephesus become the missionaries' bases of operation to evangelize the surrounding regions. Paul has a long (and sometimes tempestuous) relationship with the church at Corinth, which suffers from the kinds of problems typical of those who convert from a pagan environment of immorality and idolatry.

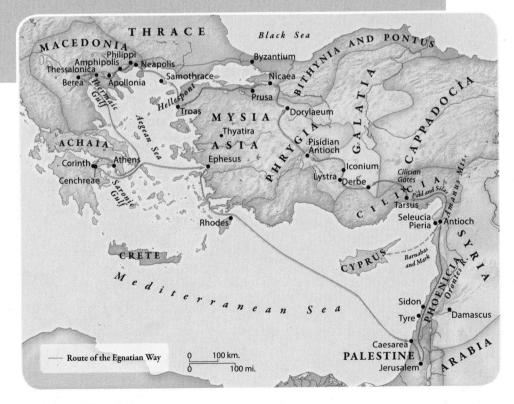

Paul's second missionary journey ca. AD 49–52 (Acts 15:36–18:22)

What if God is only as far away as we are willing to turn toward Him?

4 *actions*

What actions develop the story in this verse? What is happening in this verse? To whom?

5 *outcome*

What is God saying to me today? How do I apply this to my life?

1 *verse* What verse am I mapping? What key themes or specific words are speaking to me today?

2 *design* ———————— *develop* **3**

What different translations make up the design for this verse? Underline key phrases or words repeated.

What is the Hebrew or Greek meaning for the underlined phrases or words?

4 *actions*

What actions develop the story in this verse? What is happening in this verse? To whom?

5 *outcome*

What is God saying to me today? How do I apply this to my life?

1 *verse*   What verse am I mapping? What key themes or specific words are speaking to me today?

2 *design* ——————————————— *develop* **3**

What different translations make up the design for this verse? Underline key phrases or words repeated.

What is the Hebrew or Greek meaning for the underlined phrases or words?

session

6

The Feast

*One night the Lord spoke to Paul in a vision: "Do not be afraid;
keep on speaking, do not be silent. For I am with you, and no one is
going to attack and harm you, because I have many people in this city."*

ACTS 18:9–10

OPENING REFLECTION

It's a dream scenario for what we've been studying—finding a haven that has exactly what we need to study the Word, when we need it. Verse mapping is about unlocking the abundance of God's Word that is there waiting for us—gathering with Him, learning from the Holy Spirit, and stepping out on our story road to share what He's done in our lives.

We look at the story of the journey it's believed Luke participated in, as he traveled with the apostle Paul taking the gospel of Jesus Christ across the Aegean Sea into Macedonia. It's on this second missionary journey that scholars believe Luke traveled with Paul, as Acts 16:10 ushers in a language shift from "they" to "we." While this could be a stylistic choice, it's believed that Luke is now documenting firsthand accounts that he himself witnessed. It's as if his role changed from historical author to travel journalist.

This week, we enter a time of feasting—where the Word is abundant, and instead of ending, a new journey begins . . .

What if the feast table was always set, and the hungry were always fed to full? Can we come back to feast on God's Word, and be assured of His presence?

FEASTING AND GETTING STARTED

Welcome back for session six of *Acts: Feasting on the Abundance of God's Word.*

This may be our final session to gather for video stories, but it's not the end of studying God's Word together. Before we wrap up this journey through the book of Acts, come back together and discuss one of the following questions:

- *What verse(s) did you select to map, and why? How did it go?*

- *What areas of your heart did the Holy Spirit prompt you to entrust Him with this week? Where were the places He pursued you in a new way?*

FEASTING: VIDEO STORY

Play the video segment for session six. As you watch the final installment of our book of Acts story, follow the verse mapping guide points starting on the next page and refer to the completed map on pages 118–119. Take brief notes or record questions that might lead you to further research in your independent study time this week and in your continued study time.

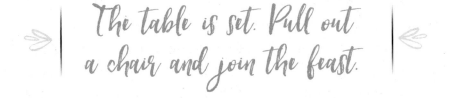

The table is set. Pull out a chair and join the feast.

Notes

 verse

What stands out in these verses:

> After Paul preaches in Thessalonica, and (with a less enthusiastic response) in Athens, he comes to Corinth. The Holy Spirit provides assurance, through a vision, that even though the persecution has been fierce in some places, the city would be a haven for Paul to speak the truth of the gospel.

> The Holy Spirit outlines what Paul is to do in Corinth—saying that Paul shouldn't be so afraid that he would turn away (or flee) from God's presence. Instead, he should keep speaking out, and he will be under God's protection IF he stays in His presence.

② design

> The Holy Spirit tells Paul that though he may be feeling fear and discouragement, he should "keep on speaking, do not be silent" (NIV).

> Other translations continue these words of instruction with, "Don't let anyone intimidate or silence you" (MSG), and, "Go on speaking and do not be silent" (NASB).

> The promise from the Holy Spirit (NIV): "For I am with you, and no one is going to attack and harm you, because I have many people in this city."

Other translations confirm this promise to Paul with, "I'm with you and no one is going to be able to hurt you" (MSG) and, "I am with you, and no man will attack you in order to harm you" (NASB).

③ *develop*

In the Greek, *phobeó* (S. 5399) means "to fear, dread; to be terrified." More than fear, the root of this word means to have such fear that a person would turn away, or flee, from something or someone.

In the Greek, *phobos* (S. 5401) is commonly used in Scripture to refer to a reverential type of fear (such as, of God), but more often in a negative way, to mean withdrawing from the Lord and His will.

The Greek word for the phrase "keep on speaking" is *laleó* (S. 2980), meaning "to talk; speak or say." It also means "chatter" in Classical Greek, but the New Testament uses the more dignified meaning of the word.

In the phrase "no one is going to attack and harm you" (NIV), the word for "attack" in the Greek is *epitithémi* (S. 2007), meaning "to place or put upon; to beat." The Holy Spirit is saying to us all that if we stay in God's presence and continue to speak the truth of the gospel, we've got a holy shield covering all points of our person.

4 *actions*

How God assures we can have CONFIDENCE in Him and continue in His will:

DON'T TURN AWAY: The Holy Spirit tells Paul not to be so fearful of what he'll encounter in Corinth that he withdraws from God's presence there (Acts 18:9)

KEEP SPEAKING OUT: The Holy Spirit tells Paul to continue to speak of the gospel; he's assured safety (Acts 18:10)

STAY IN HIS PRESENCE: The Holy Spirit tells Paul he's under God's protection IF he stays in His presence (Acts 18:10)

Paul stayed in Corinth for a year and a half—under God's protective haven—teaching the Word of God (Acts 18:11)

5 *outcome*

The more we seek God, speak of Him, and adopt fearlessness in our study time in His Word, the less we will be so afraid that we flee—or give up on God's presence

④  *What if the feast table was always set, and the hungry were always fed to full? Can we come back to FEAST on God's Word, and be assured of His presence?*

How God assures we can have CONFIDENCE in Him, and continue in His will:

- **DON'T TURN AWAY:** *Holy Spirit tells Paul not to be so fearful of what he'll encounter in Corinth that he withdraws from God's presence there* (Acts 18:9)

- **KEEP SPEAKING OUT:** *Holy Spirit tells Paul to continue to speak of the gospel, he's assured safety* (Acts 18:10)

- **STAY IN HIS PRESENCE:** *Holy Spirit tells Paul he's under God's protection IF he stays in His presence* (Acts 18:10)

Paul stayed in Corinth for a year and a half—under God's protective haven—teaching the Word of God (Acts 18:11)

⑤ *outcome* ————————————————

The more we seek God, speak of Him, and adopt fearlessness in our study time in His Word, the less we will be so afraid that we flee—or give up on God's presence.

① *verse* — ACTS 18:9–10 (NIV)

One night the Lord spoke to Paul in a vision: <u>"Do not be afraid</u>; keep on speaking, do not be silent. For I am with you, and no one is going to <u>attack</u> and harm you, because I have many people in this city."

② *design*

- **NKJV:** *"Now the Lord spoke to Paul in the night by a vision, <u>'Do not be afraid</u>, but <u>speak</u>, and do not keep silent; for I am with you, and no one will <u>attack</u> you to hurt you; for I have many people in this city.'"*

develop ③

- **AFRAID**—*phobeó (S. 5399)*

    "to fear, dread; to be terrified"

    From the Greek *phobos* (S. 5401), used in Scripture: "withdrawing from the Lord and His will"

- **SPEAK**—*laleó (S. 2980):*

    "to talk; speak or say"

    Also a "chatter" in Classical Greek, but New Testament uses more dignified meaning of the word.

- **ATTACK**—*epitithémi (S. 2007):*

    "to place or put upon; to beat"

From the Video

You step through the house to the back doors—French doors, oversized with dark wood and glass panes to greet you, and iron-scroll handles. You reach for the doors and just push them open at the center . . . and you're washed in sunlight that floods your view.

A tree, knotted and aged, with limbs reaching like arms over a long, rugged wood table—mismatched chairs mark the place settings, enough room for fifty or sixty guests or more . . . you can't see its end. And on this table are chargers with crusty bread. And bowls of figs and dates. There are pitchers for pouring, goblets for drinking.

You walk to the table. Find your name-card. Pull out a chair and sit down. More guests are about to arrive, but you have your own place setting. You were invited—expected and wanted. And as you sit, and shake out the napkin in your lap, you find the list of needs and wants that had once been so important, are silver, and china, and gold, at a table that has no need for them. You've been here before, and you'll come again.

The feast is about to begin.

FEAST TABLE: DISCUSSION

Take a few moments with your group to discuss the story you just watched and explore these concepts in Scripture.

1. Think about the culture of Corinth during the first-century, where idolatry and immorality were rampant. Why would the Holy Spirit send Paul to preach in this challenging environment, right after he'd experienced discouragement from preaching in Athens? Discuss how God can turn our discouraging experiences into triumphant ones.

---

2. Select a volunteer to read Acts 18:12–21 aloud to the group. After spending a year and a half in Corinth, Paul's ministry continues in the province of Achaia, but not without friction. How does Paul handle the challenges there, and later, in Ephesus? Did the discouragement he may have experienced in Athens prevent him from teaching God's Word in his later experiences? Discuss Paul's response to God's call on his life.

_____

_____

_____

3. Select another volunteer to read Isaiah 21:1–10 aloud to the group. How, like Isaiah's prophecy, are we called to be watchmen—those who speak out the good news about Jesus? In what ways does God's Word encourage us in this task?

_____

_____

_____

4. In today's video story, Kristy shared a dream of a backyard feast table, with place settings already laid out, and hills of abundance available to fill the table for every feast to come. How is God's Word abundant in this way—providing us everything we need, when we need it, without end? If we've never truly feasted on the Word before, how can we do it for the first time?

_____

_____

_____

Define "fear." What does it mean to you to "flee from His presence"?

_____

_____

_____

If given a feast table of your own, who would fill the chairs around you? Who are the key influences in your life to keep you encouraged in your faith journey?

_____

_____

_____

_____

_____

_____

_____

_____

FEAST TABLE: GROUP ACTIVITY

For this activity, each participant will need a Bible, pens/markers, or a smart device (such as a phone or tablet).

- Using a Bible or Bible app on a smart device, look up two additional translations of Acts 18:9–10, and record them on the completed map on pages 118–119.

- To continue your verse mapping journey, pray as a group and select one verse you'll map from Acts 21–28 in individual study time this week. And talk about gathering around the feast table again after this study is over. A coffee shop corner, a Bible, a notebook and pens, and friends with open hearts . . . it's all you need to keep going.

FEAST TABLE: CLOSING PRAYER

Every verse mapping experience begins and ends with prayer.

We end session six the same way we began—praying that Jesus would be our encourager when we have fears enough to flee, and our defender when we stay. Whether it's a six-week journey or a daily seat at a backyard feast table, we pray for more of Jesus.

We pray for the Word to be opened, and the feast to never end.

They devoted themselves to the apostles' teaching and to fellowship, to the breaking of bread and prayer. . . . And the Lord added to their number daily those who were being saved.
(ACTS 2:42, 47)

INDIVIDUAL STUDY

The Feast

One night the Lord spoke to Paul in a vision: "Do not be afraid; keep on speaking, do not be silent. For I am with you, and no one is going to attack and harm you, because I have many people in this city."

ACTS 18:9–10

FEAST: INDIVIDUAL STUDY INVITATION

Not everyone will take a place at this feast. Sometimes, discouragement may battle to keep you away. Surprised?

This week, you'll find that adversity has a place card at the feast too. The table doesn't turn away troubles in Acts 21–28. In fact, they come in the form of warnings (21:1–4), arrests (21:26–36), perilous voyages (27:13–38), and even persecution (28:30–31) for the apostles who dared pull out a chair at a righteous table.

But it's not what you think.

You're not going to mingle with the tough times; instead, you're going to watch as the King sits at the head of this table and wrangles the enemy into submission. You're going to feast on the Word. To make study your oxygen and Christ your breath, so that when adversity does show up to the party . . . you're ready. You're armed. You're full.

You've come too far to turn back now. Through fellowship with your spiritual family—and the Holy Spirit whom you now know like the back of your hand—don't give up. Don't go hungry. Don't forget this journey you've mapped. Because abundance isn't a one-time bash; this feast never ends.

Fill your plate . . . and come back for more.

Read

➤ ACTS 21 — 28 ≺

Pray. Your table is set. Ask the Holy Spirit to pull out a chair and join you there. Prepare your heart for feasting on His Word. You've been given an open-ended invitation to the dinner party, so get your pen ready . . . the feast is about to begin.

Read Acts 21–28. Adversity comes in different forms—this week, in Paul's discouragement in his calling. We're called to communion with Christ, but that doesn't mean the troubles of this earthly life will fizzle and fade if we're feasting on the Word. But the hope here is to not keep silent. To not fear. To not give up on the invitation and give away our place at the feast table. Because this journey—the feast of the Word of the living God—it's ongoing. And we need to be there.

Verse mapping is about unlocking the abundance of God's Word that's there waiting for us—gathering with Him, learning from Him, and gathering to share what He's done in our lives. We close this study with this kind of feast-until-FULL invitation. The chairs are filled, and we pray this will be the first of many feasts to enjoy as we surrender our lives to Jesus, and find we're continually fed by the Word.

When you've finished mapping your verses this week, turn to the "Story Road through Acts" section, located behind your blank maps. This will be the space to see your story mapped out. You'll find space to record the journey you've been on—to document the outcomes and lay out the entire map you've encountered in the book of Acts. Gather your verses and your outcomes, and see for yourself how intimately your heavenly Father is involved in each chapter of your story!

Study Support Examples

Information you might find in your research . . .

22:30–23:11 *Paul Before the Sanhedrin.* The commander (Lysias, see 23:26; 24:22) decides that the best way to understand the charges against Paul is to bring him before the Sanhedrin, the Jewish high court. This is a dangerous situation for Paul since this is the same body that condemned Jesus (Luke 22:66–71; 23:18,23).

23:1 I have fulfilled my duty. Translates a Greek word that comes from a root meaning "live as a citizen." Though a Roman citizen, Paul's citizenship is in God's kingdom (Phil 3:20).

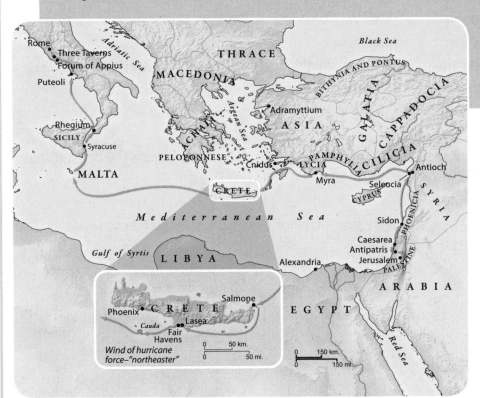

Paul's journey to Rome ca. AD 59–60 (Acts 27:1–28:16)

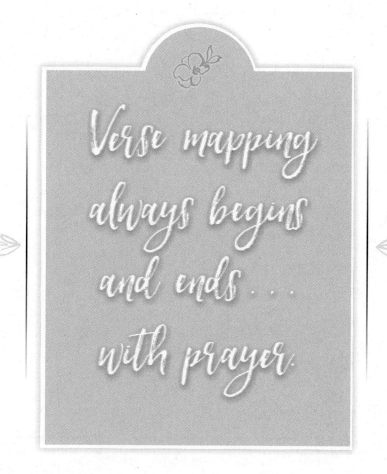

Verse mapping
always begins
and ends . . .
with prayer.

4 *actions* What actions develop the story in this verse? What is happening in this verse? To whom?

5 *outcome*

What is God saying to me today? How do I apply this to my life?

1 *verse*   What verse am I mapping? What key themes or specific words are speaking to me today?

2 *design* ———————————— *develop* **3**

What different translations make up the design for this verse? Underline key phrases or words repeated.

What is the Hebrew or Greek meaning for the underlined phrases or words?

4 *actions* What actions develop the story in this verse? What is happening in this verse? To whom?

5 *outcome*

What is God saying to me today? How do I apply this to my life?

1 *verse* What verse am I mapping? What key themes or specific words are speaking to me today?

2 *design* ──────────────── *develop* 3

What different translations make up the design for this verse? Underline key phrases or words repeated.

What is the Hebrew or Greek meaning for the underlined phrases or words?

Verse mapping reveals our personal story roads with the Holy Spirit, just as it reveals deep truths in Scripture.

STORY ROAD THROUGH

Acts

Verse mapping reveals our personal story roads with the Holy Spirit, just as it reveals deep truths in Scripture. It's going to happen in the moments of spontaneity—dependent on the Holy Spirit's direction—and in the journeys that result from your curiosity in study.

STORY ROAD INSTRUCTIONS

Write each verse we mapped through our study in the book of Acts. Starting with Acts 2:1–4, include every verse Kristy mapped in her teaching, the verses your group mapped together, and those verses you mapped in your self-study time:

Rewrite the Outcome statement from each map through our study in the book of Acts. (Look back, starting with *"Acts is a portrait of COMMUNITY among believers + UNITY with the Holy Spirit. We have the same access to the Holy Spirit that the disciples did, and the same empowering actions for the church to grow"*, include each outcome from Kristy's teachings, the outcome from each of your group maps, and each outcome from your self-study maps.)

Read over your entire journey—the outcomes that you'll refer back to over time. What message has the Holy Spirit revealed to you? Where has God breathed truth into your life, and how will you use that truth to impact this season? Remember, God meets you every time you engage Him on your story road, and He longs to walk every step of the journey alongside you!

Return to these truths. Come back to the Word with this approach. It's personal, crafted from His heart to yours. And it's not meant to stay in a study guide that gets tucked away on a shelf. Imagine you're at that backyard feast table—the one that's set for you, and where Christ welcomes you back. We wouldn't want to leave our chair empty!

This may be our last gathering, but that's not where the discipleship ends.

video maps

What are the (6) Scripture verses we mapped in the video stories? Write them here:

VERSE(S)

_____

_____

_____

_____

_____

_____

_____

group maps

What are the Scripture verses I mapped together with my group? Write them here:

VERSE(S)

_____

_____

_____

_____

_____

_____

What are the (6) Outcomes from mapping in the video stories?
Write them here:

OUTCOME STATEMENTS

What are the (6) Outcomes from mapping with my group?
Write them here:

OUTCOME STATEMENTS

my maps

What are the Scripture verses I mapped in self-study with the Holy Spirit? Write them here:

VERSE(S)

_____

_____

_____

_____

_____

— my map pin —

What has the Holy Spirit taught me in these 6 weeks? Sum up the destination as a pin on a map. Make it one word . . . a phrase . . . or an impact statement—whatever the heart of my journey, I'm committing to write it down and live it out. It's my story road right now!

What are the (6) Outcomes from mapping in self-study with the Holy Spirit? Write them here:

OUTCOME STATEMENTS

VERSE MAPPING STUDY PLANS
Book of Acts

Ready to feast again? Bring your verse mapping journal and gather with God in a new mapping journey! Feasting on the Abundance study plans for the book of Acts are here:

on MIRACLES:

- Acts 2:1–4
- Acts 5:19–20
- Acts 9:36–42
- Acts 12:7
- Acts 16:17–19
- Acts 20:9–12

on PRAYER:

- Acts 1:13–14
- Acts 8:15–16
- Acts 10:2–6
- Acts 11:5–9
- Acts 14:22–23
- Acts 22:17–21

on MINISTRY:

- Acts 4:29
- Acts 6:3–4
- Acts 13:2–3
- Acts 16:6–10
- Acts 23:11
- Acts 27:13–26

verse mapping

Reference and Resource Guide

RESOURCES TO HELP YOU STUDY THE BIBLE LIKE NEVER BEFORE

BOOKS

- *The NKJV Study Bible, 2nd Edition* (Thomas Nelson), by Earl D. Radmacher (editor), Ronald B. Allen (editor), H. Wayne House (editor)

- *NIV Chronological Study Bible* (Thomas Nelson)

- *NIV Biblical Theology Study Bible* (Zondervan), D. A. Carson (general editor)

- *The NIV Exhaustive Bible Concordance, Third Edition: A Better Strong's Bible Concordance* (Zondervan), by John R. Kohlenberger III

- *Mounce's Complete Expository Dictionary of Old and New Testament Words* (Zondervan), by William D. Mounce (general editor)

- Concordance, if other biblical translations are preferred (NASB, KJV, MSG, etc.)

- Other Bible studies—these books/study guides that are gathering dust on the shelves could be a gold mine of information when researching. Get them out and use them!

WEBSITES

- BibleGateway.com—free biblical translations, Hebrew/Greek lexicon, commentaries, concordance(s), biblical dictionaries

- BibleHub.com—great word search site, Hebrew/Greek lexicon

- Logos.com—free and paid in-depth biblical resource site

- YouTube.com—videos of sites/locations being researched

*ALWAYS utilize references/websites that come from reputable sources (i.e., NOT an online crowd-sourcing encyclopedia). It is okay to use whatever websites pop up in a Google search—as long as they contain evidence you can confirm. Approved websites could be, for example: university/seminary websites, or sites that contain articles from recognized research/news sources (History.com, Smithsonian, National Geographic, museums or historical institutions, etc.).

HISTORY BOOKS AND MAPS

Your local library can be an invaluable resource for:

- Greco-Roman art, archaeology, and history books

- Maps and in-depth historical context on life and culture in a first-century Roman world

- Anything that includes timelines, maps, etc. of the ancient world will add to your research

The point of all of this is to **think like a researcher.** *Be curious. Ask questions. Dig for answers. Don't just accept an answer—use it as a springboard to research on your own.*

SMALL GROUP OR CHURCH MEMBERS/LEADERS

- Someone who is seminary trained by education/vocation

- Someone who has walked with Jesus for many years—even in ministry—and may have valuable insight into the topic you're researching

- A member who has studied Hebrew/Greek (wowza, if you do!)—or Jewish culture

- Someone who learned what you're discussing in another Bible study

Bottom line—use the resources/sphere of influence within your reach!
ASK QUESTIONS. Own your faith in Jesus; the learning is up to you. :-)

Community Connections

Need more help? Go to versemapping.com or search the following social media hashtags to find other mappers who've shared their mapping journeys online. You'll find support and collaboration in a space that's always available.

#VerseMapping

#VerseMapclub

#GoandMakeChallenge (community maps from *Luke: Gathering the Goodness of God's Word*)

#FeastandFullChallenge (community maps from *Acts: Feasting on the Abundance of God's Word*)

Acknowledgments

When I picture a feast table—a rugged, backyard dream that became this verse mapping journey—I see rows of chairs that are no longer empty. I see place-settings that are filled, smiles that are warm, and a celebration dinner that couldn't have been if not for those gathered around this project.

For the friends who believed in this journey enough to invite us into it: John Raymond, Rachelle Gardner, Daisy Hutton . . .

For the friends and mentors who helped set the stage and lay the table: Katherine and Sarah, Beth, Jeane, Colleen, Bex, Allen, Sharon, Maggie, Eileen, Marlene, Kerry, Joyce, Kelli, Gary and Lanette . . .

For the incredible production team who saw to every detail of this feast in the Word: Mark Weising, Sara Riemersma, Brookwater Films, 52 Watt Studios, Robin Crosslin, and Greg Clouse . . .

For the beloved who sit closest at the table: Rick and Linda, Jenny, Jeremy, Brady, Carson, and Colt . . .

And for the One who pulls out the chair and waits for us . . .

. . . You showed up. You gave. You stayed and you changed everything about the journey. For that—*and for you*—I am profoundly grateful. I love you.